Ten things
they never told me
about Jesus

Ten things
they never told me
about Jesus

… a beginner's guide to a larger Christ

John L. Bell

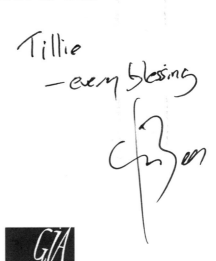

GIA Publications, Inc.
Chicago

ISBN 978-1-57999-793-9
G-7785

Published and distributed in North America by GIA Publications, Inc.
7404 S. Mason Ave., Chicago, IL 60638 www.giamusic.com

Printed by GIA Publications, Inc.

All quotations of Scripture, unless indicated otherwise, are from
The Revised English Bible
© 1989, Oxford University Press and Cambridge University Press.

Contents

Introduction

Not many people know that Jesus:

1. was left-handed;
2. had lost most of his teeth before he began his ministry;
3. smoked a type of cigar made from a desert plant called *pteugia*;
4. suffered from asthma;
5. had a childhood romance with the daughter of an Egyptian prince;
6. shared the same blood group as Judas Iscariot;
7. cured Pontius Pilate's wife of bulimia;
8. spoke fluent Latin;
9. based the Good Samaritan parable on his experience of being mugged;
10. sang tenor in his local synagogue choir.

The reason that such things are unknown is that none of them is true—which, I hope, cannot be said about what is included in this book, although some of the chapter headings might not immediately suggest a self-evident truth.

The Western church, in its understanding of Jesus, has suffered from three disorders.

1. There has been an imbalanced representation of Jesus as a passive person both in liturgical language and in graphic depiction. This is undoubtedly because the two major icons—the baby in arms and Christ on the cross—are static images inviting meditation, as distinct from dynamic images encouraging action. To some extent, there is an inevitability about the concentration of artistic and poetic energy on the

birth and death of Jesus, but they should not be allowed to eclipse the life. Phrases like "from the cradle to the cross" have tended to diminish the significance of the incarnate ministry; and films such as *The Passion of the Christ* give the impression that the crucifixion of Jesus had little to do with what went before.

There are, of course, two major statements that encourage this lack of investment in the life and ministry of Jesus. They are called the Apostles' and the Nicene Creeds. However they may be excused on grounds that they were not offering a brief biography of Jesus, but rather trying to define the faith of the church.

Having said that, the simple truth remains that we cannot understand either the Incarnation or the Cross unless we understand the life. Jesus was not simply "born to die." Nor did his death happen in isolation from the three-year public ministry he pursued; rather it happened precisely because of what he said and did in those three years.

It is in the developing world that both the iconography and the language of worship more easily celebrate a larger Christ whose humanity is explicit, rather than the diminished savior of much Western art and liturgy.

2. In some communities Jesus has been seen through the eyes of Paul as if the former were a minor prophet and the latter the Messiah. Paul actually says very little about Jesus' life and ministry. And when he does, it is sometimes obscure.

Take, for example, 1 Timothy 6:13—

> Now in the presence of God, who gives life to all things, and of Jesus Christ, who himself made that noble confession in his testimony before Pontius Pilate ...

What was the noble confession Jesus made? The synoptic Gospels (Mark, Matthew and Luke) all indicate that Jesus said nothing before Pilate.

On the other hand, Paul makes frequent mention of the crucifixion and the resurrection. That is when he is working out their theological implications. But where does he quote Jesus' sayings, allude to Jesus' parables, mention the people Jesus associated with, refer to any of Jesus' miracles?

In his defense, it is important to say that because Paul wrote letters and not Gospels, he was probably presuming that those to whom he wrote already knew the basic information regarding Jesus' life. But in the twenty-first century, this is something we cannot presume and therefore Paul must be read through Jesus and not vice versa.

When I was giving a lecture series, trying out some of the themes contained in this volume, an evidently disillusioned retired pastor asked, "Shouldn't we just forget about the Gospels and believe in Jesus as depicted by St. Paul?" I was quite shocked, and responded, "Sir, I couldn't disagree with you more. If we are inviting people to follow Jesus, we are not asking them to subscribe to a theological understanding of his life. We are asking people to join him on a journey, and for that to happen we have to know the details of what he did, so that we and others can follow."

But perhaps the reticence of the questioner came not from the Bible but from "learned debate."

3. For more than a century there has been a "Quest for the Historical Jesus," an attempt to discover from the admittedly fragmentary evidence of the Gospels what he actually did, what he actually said, and what in the Gospel records

might be the musings or commentary of the early Christian community. In the twentieth century the "Jesus Seminar" in America has involved generations of New Testament scholars using all the analytical tools of linguistics, semantics, social science and philosophy to try to find the essential core of Jesus' life and message.

There is no reason why scholars should be discouraged from this pursuit, even if the conclusions that some reach might seem to encourage agnosticism more than faith. The danger of believing that all the clues and answers lie in the academy is commented on in a collection of dialogues between N. T. Wright and Marcus J. Borg. Wright's chapter "Knowing Jesus: Faith and History" observes:

> The guild of New Testament studies has become so used to operating with a hermeneutic of suspicion that we find ourselves trapped in our own subtleties. If two ancient writers agree about something, that proves that one of them got it wrong. If they seem to disagree, that proves that one or both are wrong.
>
> (Wright, *The Meaning of Jesus,* 18)

Here, we do not go down that road. While I am quite happy to admit that there may be amendments or additions in the biblical text to Jesus' original words and actions, I am also keen to suggest that such things would not be casual. They would be based on information or reflection that, to the early church, seemed totally consonant with the will of God and life of Jesus.

Here, I invite readers to take the Gospel text as a whole and ask why certain themes appear with a regularity that has rarely been acknowledged. Perhaps the most immediate example of this is the fondness Jesus has both for eating and for talking about food. Extricate such references from the Gospels and the four books would be full of holes. Yet, with the exception of the Eucharist, table fellowship and food is not central to Christian witness today, except where it is seen as a necessary response to starvation—which is not the context in which Jesus speaks and breaks bread.

In the Bibliography is a list of books of a more academic variety, which readers may wish to consult. They do not come from one theological stable, and therefore provide a balanced diet. This volume in no way competes with their intentions. Rather, it is aimed at offering the general reader, the curious spectator, and the enthusiast for Christian faith the possibility to find much in the life of Christ to encourage and deepen discipleship.

—John L. Bell
May 2009

This book is dedicated to the memory of Gary Binnie, a young man who spent most of his life in care or in prison. He was a believer who at times doubted God for good reason. He had one of the keenest intellects I have ever encountered, and a potential for scholarship and kindness that the penal system failed to recognize. He was never "prepared for freedom" and sadly, when he was in sight of a new life and a recovered faith, he died. Some of this book owes its genesis and inspiration to correspondence we shared during ten years of his incarceration. His name deserves to be remembered on earth, for it is surely recognized in heaven.

Dedicated to the memory of
Gary Binnie
(1975–2008)

"Free at last"

Acknowledgments

There is nothing here which has not been road-tested and amended after conversation and further reflection. To name individuals would risk turning this short paragraph into something resembling pages torn from a telephone directory. So, more generally, I thank those responsible for inviting me to preach or speak to congregations, seminaries and conferences in North America, Australia and the United Kingdom in the years 2005 to 2008 when the substance of this book was taking shape. Thanks also is due to Greenbelt Festivals and Holy City (a monthly ecumenical event in Glasgow), where some ideas expressed here in words were also reflected in liturgy.

I am grateful as well to Jan Michael and Paul Clarke whose wonderful hospitality over the last two decades during summer weeks in Amsterdam has enabled me to prepare this book and many other articles and resources which would never otherwise have seen the light of day. And, as ever, with my colleagues in the Wild Goose Resource Group of the Iona Community, we are glad to acknowledge the patience, professionalism and helpfulness of the Wild Goose Publications staff, particularly the diligence of Sandra Kramer, the Publishing Manager, whose editing has prevented untold embarrassments.

I also wish to thank Michael Boschert of GIA Publications for his meticulous care in preparing this edition for North America. Not only did he correct defective references in the UK edition, but he also prevented North American readers from puzzling over British vernacular expressions.

Chapter one

Skeletons in the cupboard

A chance meeting

She was probably about 27, but she looked older. She had a kindly face, an interested face, but also a face that either hid stories or wanted to tell them. Or both. And we were having coffee in a church hall where it seemed that everybody knew each other apart from us.

So we fell into a conversation about nothing very consequential, until I asked her what she thought of the service we had just attended. It was an Anglican parish Eucharist, one Sunday morning during Advent. What had particularly impressed her was the very item about which I felt a little dubious. It was unusual, well rehearsed and clearly presented. But I wasn't as sure of its value as she seemed to be.

What was at issue was the reading of Jesus' genealogy as contained in the first chapter of Matthew's Gospel, sometimes disparagingly referred to as "The Begats":

Abraham begat Isaac;
and Isaac begat Jacob;
and Jacob begat Judah and his brethren.

As a child I had never thought it had anything to do with sex, though I should have known. For when I asked my Sunday School teacher what a "begat" was, she told me I'd understand when I was older. It was a bit like Mary. In the King James Version of the Bible, she was "great with child." I never suspected for a moment that she was pregnant.

15

At any rate, this rather dull run of 15 verses, which is full of awkward names for those unfamiliar with the ancient Hebrew world, was read by five people. Most of the begats were read by a man who stood at a lectern at the front of the church. But whenever he came to a woman's name—of which there are four, not counting Mary the mother of Jesus—a woman stood up in the middle of the congregation and began to talk about the person named as if she were a close friend.

It had always puzzled me that with all the begatting that went on, only four women were named as co-partners in procreation. Sarah, the ninety-year-old first matriarch is never given a mention. It is as if Abraham produced Isaac all on his own. Every patriarch's wife remains incognito except these four. As far as I can remember, this is what was said about them:

The truth behind the titles

Reader:
Judah was the father of Perez and Zarah (their mother was Tamar).

Woman 1:
Let me tell you about Tamar.

She married the oldest son of a widower called Judah. The boy's name was Er. But, for whatever reason, God considered Er to be wicked and so he died before they had any children.

Then Tamar, following an old custom, married the next in line, who was called Onan. He practiced coitus interruptus to avoid her conceiving, so God did away with him as well.

There was a third son, called Shelah, but as Judah had lost two sons to Tamar, and feared he'd lose a third, he prevented any further matrimony.

This left Tamar in a bit of a fix. She wouldn't be accepted by the Hebrew community because she hadn't produced any heir to continue Judah's line. And she possibly wouldn't have been welcomed back in her own community as she was no longer a virgin bride.

So, what could she do to secure both her own future and descendants for her father-in-law?

She decided on a very risky ploy. She dressed up like a cheap tart and sat at a crossroads where she gave the come-on to her father-in-law when he passed by. He didn't recognize her and had sex with her. He had no money with him to pay for services rendered, but he left a couple of personal items with her as a pledge, and he promised to send a man to redeem them with an appropriate monetary payment.

When he got round to paying his debt, the man he sent said that there was no sign of any floozy at the designated crossroads.

As time went on, Judah heard a rumor that his daughter-in-law had been playing the whore. Knowing that this would bring disgrace on the good name of his family, he ordered that she should be burned at the stake.

As she was being led to the place of execution, she let slip that she was pregnant, and that the father of her child could be indentified by the personal items he had left in her safekeeping.

17

Judah immediately recognized that he was the father of the unborn child, stopped the execution and took Tamar to be his wife.

* * *

Reader:

Salmon was the father of Boaz (his mother was Rahab).

Woman 2:

Let me tell you about Rahab.

She was a prostitute who lived in a city called Jericho.

This was one of the cities that was on a list of locations to be conquered by Joshua, then the leader of the Israelites who were trying to settle in Canaan, which they believed to be the Promised Land.

Joshua sent two men to reconnoitre the city. Once inside they decided to stay in Rahab's house. But the city authorities, made aware that two Israelite spies had visited the local brothel, demanded that Rahab hand them over. She said that they had indeed paid a visit, but had left before the city gates were closed for the night.

Actually, she had hidden them in the rafters of her house where they could not be detected should a search be mounted.

The next day she told the two men that she had a good idea of their intentions and that she was convinced that the God of the Israelites was able to do whatever he wanted. So she asked that if they attacked the city, she and her family might be spared.

The men agreed to secure her safety during the attack as long as she didn't betray them. She agreed to this and let them out of the city by a rope from her window.

The understanding was that when the city was being attacked, she should hang a piece of scarlet cord from the same window through which the spies had escaped. That would be a sign to the Israelite troops to rescue all who were in that household.

This happened, and Rahab eventually married into the Israelite community.

* * *

Reader:
Boaz was the father of Obed (his mother was Ruth).

Woman 3:
Let me tell you about Ruth.

She was one of two young women who married brothers, the sons of an older woman called Naomi.

Both brothers died and Naomi decided that it would be best for her to go back to her home town, which was called Bethlehem.

Ruth was insistent that she would go with Naomi whom she loved dearly. But, once there, she had to find work, and if possible find a husband through whom she'd be incorporated into the Hebrew community.

She began by gleaning what the reapers had left from harvesting the barley field. There, her youth and beauty were a distraction to the workmen. However the owner, whose name was Boaz, made sure she was not molested. He was a distant relative of her late husband, but much older than Ruth.

When Naomi discovered that Boaz was being kind to Ruth, she encouraged the girl to engage in an elaborate seduction ritual with the older man. This was successful and, in time, Ruth became his wife.

* * *

Reader:

David was the father of Solomon (his mother had been the wife of Uriah).

Woman 4:

Let me tell you about her. She was called Bathsheba. Her husband, Uriah, was a loyal soldier in King David's army.

One evening while his men were fighting a battle, David—who had remained in Jerusalem—took a stroll on his palace roof. From there he saw a very attractive woman taking a bath. He lusted after her, told servants to bring her to him and had intercourse with her, even though her menstrual period should have restricted such activity.

She—Bathsheba—became pregnant and sent word to David.

He decided that he wanted her for a wife. So he engineered to have Uriah, her husband, sent into battle in such a way that it was guaranteed he would be killed.

This happened, and Bathsheba became another wife in the royal household, but the child who had been conceived in these unusual circumstances didn't live long.

* * *

... this is virtually how the genealogy of Jesus was read. And this is what so impressed the young woman with whom I was having coffee.

I wanted to know why it had made such an impact on her. She replied, "I used to be a prostitute. But I gave that up. I'm now a Christian and I won't be going back to my old trade again. However, I have a son. He's seven now. But when he's older, I hope he comes to church and hears the Gospel read the way it was read this morning. Because one day I will tell him what I used to do. I don't want him to hear it first from anyone else. And on that day I will also want him to know that there's a place for women like me in the family tree of Jesus."

God and human deficiency

Four women with rather curious sexual histories. And four women who were not born Hebrews, but were incorporated into the Hebrew community through marriage. And they are the only ones who are named in Jesus' genealogy.

Did this happen by chance? Or was it intended by God that these names and stories should have a place in scripture because Jesus was neither to be advantaged by a pedigree of flawless ancestors nor to attract only those who were morally virtuous. The Incarnation is not about God avoiding the flaw lines in history or in humanity, but about God immersing himself in a deficient world and among fallible people because he knows that through impartial love all can be redeemed.

And perhaps people would never have found credible Jesus' claim to be truly divine and human if he had come from a pedigree of pristine piety, in which every ancestor had an unimpeachable track record.

Chapter two

A birth, not a babyfest

Nativity playtime

"I am that angel!" he said.

And everyone—adults as well as children—gasped audibly with a mixture of amusement and astonishment.

He was called Jack and he was 75, a retired taxi-driver, a recovering alcoholic and, more recently, a widower. He had no long pedigree of faith, but had become a believer after his wife had died. And he was one of a group of twelve people who met with my colleague and me over a two-year period to develop leadership potential in a local church where, minister apart, there was no adult who had gone to school past the age of fifteen.

For the two of us who were leading the group, it was an amazing experience of unlearning suppositions and discovering potentials, no more so than when, in the second year of our engagement with the congregation, we were asked to do something about Christmas.

Hitherto, as in many churches, the annual "delight" was a nativity play performed by children, more for admiring parents than for the glory of God. Usually some children forgot their lines and usually adults at the back never heard what was amusing others at the front.

Nativity plays, like many other Christmas celebrations, are reminiscence projects par excellence. They remind adults of what they once did or were or believed. I had this confirmed one Christmas Eve when preaching at Midnight Mass in St. Mary's Cathedral in Glasgow. As I began to speak, I asked those in the congregation who once had been shepherds to raise their hands. People quickly caught on, and around fifty hands were raised. Ditto for angels and wise men. There I stopped, thinking it indiscreet to ask those who once had been virgins to identify themselves.

The common belief that there is a donkey in the nativity story (something not attested to in the Gospels of Matthew or Luke) can be attributed to the fact that in childhood some people were the front and some the back ends of the hapless beast that allegedly carried Mary. Hence it is read into the story rather than discovered within the biblical witness.

There is, for many people, something of quiet personal assurance in singing again the carols learned in childhood, or in tuning in annually to "A Service of Lessons and Carols" broadcast from wherever. Even the hardest heart melts when a ten-year-old choirboy with a well-scrubbed face sings the first verse of "Once in Royal David's City."

Is there anything wrong with that? No. Not if Christmas is primarily an action replay of what we once did, an annual visit to the theme park of a (Victorian) childhood. But there *is* something wrong if this reminiscence project displaces a deeper grasp and understanding of the significance of what transpired at Bethlehem. For Christmas did not happen in the crèche of a dimly lit hall where children role-played. Christmas happened in a predominantly adult environment among people who were not at all rehearsed in the part they were allotted.

24

The real thing

This was one of the first realizations that dawned on old Jack and the other eleven people who met in Carnwadric Parish Church to prepare Christmas worship. We looked at the story and, excepting Jesus, could find no children implicitly or explicitly involved.

To put it in more graphic form, the following is a list of those normally identified when I ask unsuspecting groups of people in seminaries, as well as churches, exactly who is present in the nativity story.

Principal players:
    Mary
    Joseph
    Jesus
    Donkey
    Innkeeper
    Innkeeper's Wife
    Shepherds (usually 3)
    Wise Men (inevitably 3)

Who are surplus to requirement? The fourth, fifth and sixth. We've already dismissed the donkey. We can also get rid of the innkeeper and the innkeeper's wife since they are never mentioned. Of those remaining, we can presume that none were children or teenagers, although Mary—by legend alone— has the best claim.

Joseph is commonly presumed to be older, partly because he seems to know about divorce procedures and also because he is not around when Jesus, aged thirty, preaches in his home synagogue. The shepherds would be adult men rather than boys, if they had to keep awake at night to ward off wild animals and thieves. And as regards the Wise Men, Middle-Eastern cultures then, as now, considered wisdom as something attained not through academic degrees, but by experience, reflection and longevity.

We should, of course, add some other characters—like the principals in the occupying forces: Augustus Caesar who ordered a census, and Herod, the old and threatened king of Judaea.

But more particularly we might remember the senior citizen bookends—the retired priest Zechariah and his wife Elizabeth who, in their twilight years, became the parents of John (he would become known as the Baptist); and Simeon and Anna, two aged and devout believers who were waiting for God's promised deliverer to appear.

Christmas is about old people. That is the Gospel truth. It is consonant with the foundation story at the beginning of the Hebrew scriptures in which God calls a retired couple, Abraham and Sarah, to be the progenitors of the Hebrew race. It is as if God's vocation for the elderly is that they should be the midwives of the new thing that God is doing—an expectation and accolade sadly avoided in many churches in favor of labeling older people as resistant and reactionary.

That is why, at Carnwadric, we wrote not another nativity play, but an Advent play, presented on the Sunday before Christmas in the church by adults dotted throughout the congregation whose forward-facing pews had been rearranged to form an open quadrangle. On that day the children sat in the center and took in the story in an entirely different way. Hence the gasp when, recognizable because of his distinctive, former-beer-drinker's nose, Jack identified himself as the angel Gabriel.

When we deal with Christmas, we deal with two very different stories about Jesus. The one is based on the extended narratives at the beginning of the Gospels of Matthew and Luke. The second has to do with a seasonal cultural activity based loosely on Jesus' birth, but with accretions that have gradually taken on the status of primary elements and have substituted a trite festival of sentimentality for the deep mystery of the Incarnation.

This is the event that has no parallel in any world religion. It is the time when the Creator of heaven and earth decides, out of love for the world, to forgo the distance and safety of heaven in order to experience the risk and joy of life on earth in solidarity with humanity. This is God forgoing privilege, setting aside his glory, becoming one of the crowd and doing so in the person of a peasant girl's son.

It is the movement in the heart of God that, along with the death of Christ on the cross, should leave us speechless in our inability to comprehend why it happened for the benefit of those who—even yet—are totally unaware of its importance, and forever beyond its deserving.

So, if we are to celebrate the Incarnation with integrity rather than panache, it would be responsible to separate out the truth as it is related in the Gospels from the babyfest, which it has become.

A deeper understanding

Here, with all due deference to legitimate questions about the historical veracity of the nativity stories, I want to consider the accounts offered by Matthew and Luke as conveying truth more profound than the details of their narratives.

To illustrate this, let me take an example from Central America. Pastors and priests in countries like Nicaragua have used Liberation Theology methods to enable the stories and insights of local people to come into contact with the story of God. This is a radical departure from conventional preaching in which the ordained minister is the sole interpreter.

On one occasion, the priest read to the people how the wise men were summoned by a star to begin a journey that led to Jesus. The priest then invited people to comment on this in the light of their own insight and experience. Among several contributions, one came from an old peasant who commented:

> When God called the wise men, he sent a star. But when God called the poor shepherds, he sent a choir of angels. I think the poor must be God's favorite people.

There is both a simple logic and a profound theological perspective in this statement. It is not something that would come from a class in exegesis at any major or minor seminary. But who is to say that it is wrong? Is it not, rather, that when we deal with a story as old and revered as the nativity story, we are dealing with a parcel of truth that has an untold possibility in terms of application, meaning and resonance?

And in taking the story seriously, is it not perfectly possible that an illiterate peasant who comes to it with fondness and curiosity might discover a truth that has evaded the most learned of minds? Or is God the Lord only of the intellect and the intelligentsia?

Victorian distractions

If one asks who is responsible for the displacement of the true significance of Christmas, no small blame has to be attributed to that phalanx of hymnwriters and music publishers who, in the heady days of Victoria's reign, began to word-paint the pastiche.

There used to be a church in the west of Scotland where meticulous timing was essential for the efficacy of the watchnight service on Christmas Eve. A minute or so before midnight, the organist would begin to play "Silent Night" and when the congregation came to the words "Strikes for us now the hour of grace" (as the text is sung in Scotland), if all was going well, the steeple bell would begin to chime midnight, announcing the arrival of Christmas day.

Add to "Silent Night" the text of "O Little Town of Bethlehem" and there is further reason to suspect a total absence of noise, a hush in the world in expectation of the birth of the Messiah:

How silently, how silently the wondrous gift is given.

Poets and wordsmiths throughout history have gradually persuaded Christendom that the Incarnation of God was a silent affair, with the whole of the natural order as well as humanity observing a solemn pause in routine activity until the cry of the child in the manger indicated the coming of God into the world.

That in itself, however, is contradicted by other fond carols, which suggest that not even the trauma of birth was registered by the lungs of the Christ-child. Hence "Away in a Manger" informs us,

The cattle are lowing, the baby awakes,
but little Lord Jesus, no crying he makes.

As alluded to above, physical art does not come to our aid, but inevitably represents in the media of paint or stone an inexpressive baby born into a world of pastoral bliss.

Would it ruin our celebration of Christmas if this traditional depiction of noiseless bliss were deconstructed? Perhaps it would do us good.

There is nothing in the Bible, either in the prophetic literature or in the birth narratives, that suggests things were quiet. Quite the opposite. The context in which Mary and Joseph arrive at Bethlehem is, allegedly, that of a census requiring men to return to their birthplace along with their families for the purposes of registration. If this was indeed the situation, and if Bethlehem's hotel accommodation was as full as is reported, then the one thing that would be present in abundance would be noise.

People would be partying. School friends would be reunited. Men who had not seen each other for between five and fifty years would be identifying the change in each other's shape and foliage. Women would be gossiping about their marriage partners, their children or their lodgings. The sound of high spirits and the occasional inebriate would be more likely to percolate the air than a solemn hush.

To imagine that at a minute to midnight people put their fingers to their lips and called for silence in order that all could hear the synagogue bell and the cry of a newborn child is sheer fantasy. Apart from anything else, synagogues—as distinct from churches—did not have bell-steeples or automatic clocks that chimed the hours.

The supposed silence has to have its cover blown, for the simple reason that in order that the birth of Christ might be as natural as any birth it was important that it was surrounded by the din of the world and not silence. No one knew that the Messiah was being born, with the exception of the only two individuals recorded as being present in the birthing room, namely Mary and Joseph.

Authentic silence

The only silence that can justifiably be celebrated in the carols or nativity tableaux is that of God's anonymity. God chose to enter the world when it was unprepared to receive him, when neither the civic nor religious establishments had a clue as to what was happening, and when the only visitors immediately summoned to celebrate the event (the shepherds) were people of no standing. It had to be a busy world so that nobody would know that God was slipping in among us.

Here is the measure of God's affection for the earth and its people, that he should express solidarity with humankind by taking on the risk of birth in order to secure the salvation of the world. And in the total absence of any publicity regarding the birth of Jesus, a pattern is set, which will not be broken for thirty years.

Indeed, even in his baptism, there is no one aware of the unusual and unnecessary appearance of Jesus in the queue lining up before John. No one, excepting the Baptist himself, sees anything unusual in the thirty-year-old man who is queuing amid civil servants, soldiers, practitioners of every craft in town, backsliders and the inevitable victims of superstition. Nobody is pointing the finger and saying, "You are sinless. You don't need to be baptized as a sign of repentance!" Nobody recognized him.

31

Instead, Christ in his baptism as at his birth arrives incognito. No one but John hears a voice from heaven, no audience spots the Holy Spirit in the form of a dove. God, as is God's wont, comes in the silence of anonymity.

But back to Christmas.

More Victorian accretions and an infant's corrective

Range through the popular Victorian carols (as distinct from their older forebears) and other questionable accretions become evident—like the tradition of the shepherds bringing a lamb. It may be alluded to in Christina Rossetti's poem "In the Bleak Midwinter," but it has no place in scripture. Indeed, from a common sense angle, what would the Holy Family do with a lamb except perhaps kill it and eat it? (Oh, not in the peaceful stable surely!)

And what about the animals—none of whom are given a mention by Matthew and Luke—who gather round the crib, breathing onto the baby? Had first-century Jews no understanding of elementary hygiene and baby care?

There is in the Hebrew scriptures what at one time would have been considered a proof-text for the presence of animals in the cave or stable or cattle shed where Jesus was born. The verse in question reads:

> An ox knows its owner
> and a donkey its master's stall. *(Isaiah 1:3a)*

This, however, is a poetic allusion, not a prophecy in search of literal fulfilment.

The degree to which the babyfest overshadows over the Incarnation in popular imagination was clearly exhibited when the council of churches in the beautiful English town of Malvern asked if I would adjudicate a carol competition. It had three qualifying age groups: primary school, secondary school, and adult. Submissions all had to be set to the Welsh tune SUO GAN.

Having agreed to judge the entries, I received in due course a large package with three folders enclosing the submissions of each age group. I waited until I had a long train journey from London to Glasgow before beginning the project. By the time we had reached Crewe, I felt like asking if anyone in the compartment had antidepressants. Every carol, from that of the youngest child to the oldest adult, was full of the fond clichés and tired images from the Victorian barrel of Christmas hymnody. And I was supposed to select a first, second and third prize-winner in each category—and an overall winner!

In a wholly disconsolate state, I was about to return the three folders to the postal package in which they had come, when I found a slim envelope I had previously overlooked. It was labelled Misfits, and contained a small number of items that, in one way or another, did not fulfil the competition criteria.

Among them was this poem:

> Father God, I love you
> and your little Jesus.
> I would like to kiss him
> and give him a cuddle.
> I would share all my toys,
> and play lots of games with him.
> Bob the Builder we could play;
> we would be the best of mates.

I said to myself, "That's it. That's the only one that will be given a prize."

I then turned over the poem to find on the reverse that it was written by Master Isaac Hutchings, age three and a half. But this little boy had got it absolutely right. He would have known the Christmas story, but felt that something else was needed … the offer of friendship to a new baby.

Perhaps if I had been the late John Wilson, I would have been more reticent to judge a carol competition. He was a Methodist, a former schoolmaster and music lecturer, and arguably the leading authority on hymn tunes in twentieth-century Britain. When my colleague Graham Maule and I had two collections of songs published, he sent a totally unsolicited letter of encouragement with the open invitation to visit him at his home in Guildford, which offer was subsequently taken up.

In gratitude to him for the great shot-in-the-arm his letter had been, we decided to dedicate a forthcoming book of Christmas songs, *Innkeepers and Light Sleepers*, to John. But prior to that I wanted to ask his advice on the tricky harmonization of a beautiful Irish folk tune. When he asked what the tune was for, I rather nonchalantly said that I was thinking of putting the words of a Christmas carol to it.

"Christmas?" responded John. "I can't stand Christmas. When it comes, all I want to do is lie in bed and think about the Incarnation" … which is maybe what we all should do, at least for a few hours on December 25, and allow ourselves to marvel at God's risk, trust and surprise.

Notwithstanding their defects, I will continue to sing Christmas carols, even those that are biblically unverifiable, because at Christmas God entered into solidarity with fallible

and misguided humanity, and that should be a corrective
to any temptation to demur. But I will still look for songs
that owe more to biblical truth than to fantasy, and I will
occasionally enjoy making light of the babyfest.

With apologies to Phillips Brooks and Ralph Vaughan Williams ...

O little town of Bethlehem,
how rowdy you appear
as homecome emigrants are buoyed
by sentiment and beer.
The long-haired tearaway returns,
grandfatherly and grey,
and former glamour-pusses' pasts
emerge in all they say.

Who knows if Ned the publican,
whose rooms could take no more,
would pleasantly or angrily
greet strangers at the door?
Who knows if he had cats and dogs
around his cattle shed,
or whether robins twittered on
or even Mrs. Ned?

But if he let his stable out
to be a labor room
for some expectant teenage mum
and her embarrassed groom,
the breath and stink of tethered beasts
would set the midwives wild
if keen to minimize the risk
to Mary and her child.

And would poor shepherds, when disturbed
from midnight peace and calm,
presume a newborn baby boy
would want to hold a lamb?
And if the Magi from the East
did "enter in all three"
was it true that they, in homage,
bent a single knee?

And did the baby never cry,
and was the mother mild
when Herod sensed that he'd been duped
and let his men run wild?
And was the father pre-programmed
to take a passive part
when one old man foretold the child
would break his mother's heart?

Christ was not born at Christmas time
invoked by practiced choirs,
embraced by plastic mangers
and fulfilling our desires.
No kindergarten was his home,
no drummer-boy his page,
no earth had frozen snow on snow
when God had come of age.

Instead, on the periphery,
eccentric through decree,
the power behind the universe
was born a refugee;
a refugee from heaven above
became the world's creator,
and chose an unknown peasant girl
as host and liberator.

Chapter three

Fully equipped

Teenagers in search of truth

Several years ago, I was invited to be the conference preacher at the annual gathering of the Presbyterian Association of Musicians at Montreat, North Carolina. This event attracts up to 1400 people for each of two parallel-programmed weeks. One of the subsidiary engagements involved meeting from Monday to Friday with a group of around seventy senior high students, young people aged between 17 and 19.

The intention of the organizers was that I should deliver a series of talks, which would be recorded and available on CD. However, I managed to argue for a more interactive kind of meeting, and it was determined that, as much as possible, I would let the teenagers set the agenda.

So, on the Monday of the first week, I inquired of the group as to whether they were aware of a game called "Spin the Bottle." For the uninitiated, this is a means by which participants can try to discover untold truths about each other (although in some parts of the world, the US included, this is a game about kissing). The procedure is that one person thinks of a question that he/she would be willing to answer. It could be anything from "Have you ever cheated in an exam?" to "Have you ever inhaled?"—a favorite for those with political aspirations. A bottle is then spun and whomever it points to has to answer the question in all honesty.

The teenagers were well aware of this leisure pursuit. So I suggested that we amend the rules slightly such that when the bottle had spun and ended up pointing to someone, everyone else in the group could ask him/her one question to which an honest reply had to be given. I suggested that imagine playing with this new rule in a group of people among whom was Jesus, and that the bottle ended up pointing at him. What one question would each of us like to ask him?

I gave the teenagers time to talk about this among themselves and then called for possible questions to be put to Jesus.

Some were both unexpected and interesting. One boy wanted to ask, "What did it feel like to send out five loaves and two fishes and receive back twelve baskets of scraps?"

Another youth, doubtless predestined to achieve a PhD in systematic theology before his twenty-first birthday, wanted to know what Jesus thought of the "eschatological issue."

Being the time of *The Da Vinci Code*'s popularity, there was a range of issues regarding Jesus' sexual conduct and prowess:

Did you ever masturbate?
Did you have the hots for Mary Magdalene?
Were you gay?
Did you ever have sex?

Having raised the issues and promising to make them the subject of our discussions, I was left at the end of the first session not only with questions seeking answers, but also with the dilemma of deciding the order in which the issues would be discussed.

With the plethora of questions about Jesus' sex life, I was tempted to leave that until the last day and begin with the "eschatological issue" in the hope that it would result in a waning of interest in the seminars.

A hidden fact of (his) life

However, I determined that perhaps that which was upper-most should be dealt with first. So, the following day, when the group met, I began with some carefully chosen words. I said:

> I want to tell you something about Jesus, which probably no one has ever mentioned to you before. And what I am going to say I can reveal with complete confidence. It is simply that *[deep breath]* Jesus had a … penis.

There was a mixture of stunned silence on the part of some teenagers, and squeals of astonishment from others. In the back row a group of around six adults—the Presbyterian Thought Police—looked incredulous. I continued:

> Perhaps not everyone heard me, so I'll say it again a bit louder: Jesus had a penis.

> We don't know anything about his Achilles tendon, his tonsils, his knees or his armpits. We don't know if he had hair on his chest or a squint. But we do know for certain that he had a penis. How come?

A girl in the front row suggested in all innocence, "Because he got circumcised." "That's right," I replied, "and you don't do that to a man's thumb, do you?" "No," she replied.

There ensued an hour of fascinating conversation. It was as if liberation had been announced and people were free to say or conjecture what they wanted. We discussed what were the concomitants of agreeing that Jesus was "fully equipped."

It meant, according to some, that he must have had erections and wet dreams as he moved through puberty into adolescence. It meant that he would have experienced arousal in the presence of those to whom he felt a sexual attraction. It meant that he might have been embarrassed about his body as it—and his emotions—underwent the changes associated with moving from boyhood through adolescence into adulthood.

And, inevitably, conjecture was then made as to whether it could be presumed that he did or did not experience sexual intimacy with another person.

Jesus then and teenagers now

At this point, a whole range of existential rather than biblical or theological factors were opened for conversation. The group discovered, for example, that it would have been highly unlikely that Jesus had a bedroom of his own with a door he could lock. Because the whole family in first-century Palestine sometimes lived in one room, the kind of privatized existence, which some twenty-first-century teenagers enjoy, would not be possible. Indeed, within the Jewish community of his day, Jesus would not experience anything like the kind of teenage life that young people have today. For, at his bar mitzvah around the age of 12, he would move from the carefree world of the child into the world of adult responsibilities. There was no six-to-eight-year teenage hinterland with its own music, fashion and culture. Such a thing is a post-World War II phenomenon.

We discussed what it would be like to live without access to condoms or other methods of birth control at a time when untreatable venereal disease could lead to madness and/ or death. We talked about how young people would relate to each other in small, tight-knit communities in contrast to the seeming anonymity of a large city with motorized transportation.

And we talked about the Jewish understanding of the place of sex within a marital context and the penalties for taking a girl's virginity, as prescribed in the law of Moses.

We talked about what it would feel like to live in a society where life was not so unnecessarily sexualized as is the case today when advertisements, aimed particularly at teenagers, are heavily loaded with incentives to covet or lust.

And other issues that I had not expected were raised, such as whether the uniqueness of Jesus would have been compromised if he had had a wife or partner, with or without a child. And we pondered whether, had Jesus fathered a son or daughter, generations thereafter would have been more obsessed with tracing his descendants than fulfilling his will.

It was a fascinating conversation, substantially replicated with the same age group during the second week of the conference.

What struck me most was the earnestness of this group of high school students when their questions and conjectures were taken seriously, rather than suppressed in favor of a dogmatic lecture. I got the feeling that, at the end of it all, it was of no importance to anyone that Jesus would probably never have engaged in intimate sexual contact with a partner, committed or otherwise. What had been vindicated was that he was a real man.

There were around eighty people in all in the seminar room that first Tuesday, but it seemed by the following morning that the other 1300 people at the conference were talking about a part of Jesus' anatomy, which had hitherto been kept strictly under wraps.

A denial of full humanity

On reflection, it dawned on me that the denial of Jesus' genitalia was symptomatic of a far more pervasive emasculation of Christ that has to be reversed. Or if not emasculation, then certainly a refining of the character and manners in the one who came to show what God was truly like and to turn the tables on conventional religious respectability.

If one thinks of popular religious iconography—at least in the West—the three dominant images of Jesus to which Christian art and hymnody witness are all passive. These are the Baby in Arms, the Dying Savior, and the Redeemer Enthroned in Heaven.

The first of these deserves our current attention. It has been alluded to in Chapter Two, but it is important here to note how we rarely, if ever, see Jesus depicted as exhibiting the kind of behavior associated with most babies. He does not scream, as babies do, either for food or because they are determined to exploit the reverberant acoustic of a location such as the local church.

We do not see, hear or think of Jesus being bathed and splashing in the water, puking over his mother's allegedly blue gown, crying when put in the arms of someone strange to him, being breast-fed, pulling the wise men's beards or trying to appropriate their headgear for his own pleasure.

Such things are normal behavior in babies and toddlers, but it is a rare visual or word artist who celebrates such liveliness in Jesus. We have already noticed how "Away in a Manger" depicts Jesus as the kind of silent, motionless child whom any mother would worry about. But the confusion over Jesus' normality does not end with "no crying he makes."

Equally confusing is the curious transition from the terrestrial to the celestial realm in the space of two verses:

> I love you, Lord Jesus! Look down from the sky
> and stay by my side until morning is nigh.

Adding to the confusion over Jesus' normality, Mrs. Cecil Frances Alexander in the carol "Once in Royal David's City" suggests that this quietude that dominated Jesus' earliest days actually continued up to his bar mitzvah. Hence we are enjoined to sing:

> And through all his wondrous childhood
> he would honor and obey,
> watch and love the lowly maiden
> in whose gentle arms he lay.

Any mother confronted with such docility in her child would seek the counsel of a good pediatrician who would doubtless discourage her from cradling her ten-year-old from morning till night. Of course, Mrs. Alexander had an ulterior motive:

> Christian children all must be
> mild, obedient, good as he.

But was that ulterior motive intended to endorse the prevalent Victorian child-rearing nostrum that "little children should be seen and not heard"? Or was it to discourage children from emulating their Savior who, at the age of 12 or thereabouts, gave his parents the slip and had them hunting for him for three days in an unfamiliar city *(Luke 2:41–52)*. Perhaps if Mrs. Alexander had been more of a biblical literalist she would have concluded the verse with a different couplet:

> Christian children must abscond
> if of God they're truly fond.

The antidote for this perversion of reality is to admit that the Gospel records tell us virtually nothing about the behavior of Jesus as a baby. He is shrouded not in silence but in normality.

Only thus can he be truly human.

There are, of course, fanciful legends found in what are known as apocryphal gospels, which report alleged happenings in Jesus' early life, as when he is supposed to have turned clay birds into living creatures. But such things can be discounted, not simply because they are not witnessed to in the four Gospels contained in the New Testament, but also because they go against the grain of the incarnate Christ whose childhood was necessarily normal. Had he been recognized as an adolescent miracle-worker, or had he been celebritized as the Messiah-in-waiting, he would not have come onto the stage of human history as one who redeemed the world from the bottom up, but rather as one whose privileged past would have encouraged the opinion that he patronized the world from the top down.

One of the few revered post-Reformation hymn texts in Scotland comes from a nineteenth-century Baptist, Mary MacDonald, who lived as a crofter (tenant farmer) on the Island of Mull. She is remembered mostly because her poem *Leanabh an aigh* (which in English is entitled "Child in a Manger") was responsible for popularizing the tune BUNESSAN, a melody transcribed from the playing of a folk fiddler, and more famously paired with "Morning Has Broken."

In the United States her carol runs to four verses, but in Britain it is normally represented in a truncated form, with verse two omitted, perhaps out of a distaste for what might be (wrongly) regarded as republican or anti-royalist sentiment. It is a pity because, in conjunction with the subsequent verse

of the hymn, it appositely bears witness to the uniqueness of
Christ the King.

> Monarchs have tender,
> delicate children,
> nourished in splendor,
> > proud and gay.
> Death soon shall banish
> honor and beauty,
> pleasure shall vanish,
> > forms decay.

> But the most holy
> child of salvation
> gently and lowly
> > lived below.
> Now as our glorious
> mighty Redeemer,
> see him victorious
> > o'er each foe.

The risks of birth and life revealed

Theology and reflection on scriptural texts can help to correct
the imbalance of centuries of romanticizing the childhood of
Jesus. But more recently sociology and archaeology have come
to our aid as tools to bear witness to how the lives of children
in the first-century ancient Near East were anything but safe
and cosseted, irrespective of their pedigree.

In 1992, Bruce J. Malina and Richard L. Rohrbaugh produced
a fascinating book entitled *Social-Science Commentary on
the Synoptic Gospels*. It essentially draws on scientific and
demographic evidence to give readers an accurate picture of

life in the first century in a much more incisive way than older books about Palestine in the time of Christ.

They indicate, for example, that the birth of a child—whether in a stable or elsewhere—was a risky business for both mother and baby. At that time, one in four women died in the process of giving birth, and one in three babies suffered perinatal death.

Equally alarming is evidence that the survivors of the trauma of birth had a similarly risky infancy in front of them.

> In the cities of antiquity, nearly a third of the live births were dead before the age of six. By the mid-teens, 60 percent would have died, by the mid-twenties 75 percent, and 90 percent by the mid-forties. Perhaps 3 percent reached their sixties.
>
> (Malina & Rohrbaugh, *Social-Science Commentary*, 41)

That may begin to make sense of why in Jesus' ministry, as in that of the early church, there was particular attention paid to the widows and fatherless. There were perhaps as many—if not more—fractured as fully intact families. But the statistics also indicate how, whatever else Jesus was doing between his infancy and thirtieth birthday, he was living in a world where the risk and fragility of life were much more evident than security.

Chapter four

Christian family values?

Family Values—it's a favorite curtain-raiser and vote-winner for politicians, especially in the USA, and most especially when the adjective "Christian" prefaces it to attract the interest of those in the faith community.

So, I was keen to investigate what the Bible says about this salient issue and asked people at a conference on Iona to do the research. We split into three groups, each of which had a different aspect to consider, one Bible per person, and a list of references to start their project.

Group A was to look at the exemplars of good family values whom Jesus would discover among the patriarchs and heroes of the Jewish faith.

Group B had the responsibility of looking at the relationships Jesus had with people in his own family.

Group C was asked to attend to the specific words Jesus said about family life and deduce what they could from such utterances.

We separated for almost an hour and when we returned, members of all three groups had amusement and consternation on their faces. The reason became clear when we discussed their findings.

Ancestral exemplars

There are few, if any, men in the hierarchy of Old Testament heroes who model a sense of family responsibility that others should be encouraged to emulate.

At the start of the Jewish family tree comes Abraham, who may have shown his trust in God by being prepared to sacrifice his son Isaac, but whose fidelity to his wife Sarah has to be questioned in the light of two occasions on which he passed her off as his sister *(Genesis 12:10–16; 20:1–18)*, leading to at least one embarrassing overture. His grandson, Jacob, followed his grandfather's practice. This was after he had persuaded his hapless brother to forgo his birthright, and covered his own smooth arm with a hairy pelt in order to be given his father's blessing *(Genesis 25:29–34; 27:1–29)*.

Isaac, Abraham's son (like Samson who appears much later), enters into marriage with someone whom his father has sought for him. It is an unusual mating ritual. Whenever the unsuspecting girl Rebecca appears, Isaac immediately takes her into his tent and beds her in consolation for the loss of his mother *(Genesis 24, esp. v. 67)*.

Joseph comes from a large family where it seems that his own precocity and the jealousy of his brothers combine to ensure the disruption of normal family relations and a practiced duplicity in the reunification of the family years later *(Genesis 37 & 42)*.

Much later in the genealogy there is David who has a collection of spouses, not all of whom are happy, and who commits adultery with the wife of a loyal soldier *(2 Samuel 11)*. In his years as king, his life is threatened by the murderous intent of his son Absalom *(2 Samuel 17 & 18)*. Another son,

Solomon, the fruit of his union with Bathsheba, should have known a lot about family values, given that he had 700 wives and 300 concubines *(1 Kings 11:3)*. But he is curiously seldom quoted as a model for emulation.

Outside the Abrahamic/Davidic lineage there are men like Moses, who had a rather disruptive and disorienting childhood, having been born a Hebrew but raised in an Egyptian palace. Apart from being a murderer and a fugitive, he had a less than fulfilling relationship with his wife, who must be one of the few women in history to have made her husband a "blood-bridegroom by circumcision" *(Exodus 4:26)*.

Then there is Jephthah, a soldier and devout believer, who promised God that if he won a victory he would sacrifice the first creature that ran out of his farmyard. Presuming it might be a farm animal or even a favorite dog, he was brought up short when his daughter ran to greet the conquering hero. She spent two months in the mountains mourning her virginity, after which he subsequently sacrificed her *(Judges 11)*.

By-passing Samson, for reasons best discovered by those who want to read his full story *(Judges 14–16)*, we might light on Saul, the first anointed king of Israel. Apart from suffering from what could have been a form of schizophrenic illness, he also boiled with irrational jealousy at his son's affectionate relationship with the young David *(1 Samuel 16:14–23; 20:30–34)*.

No, there are not many good examples in his ancestry to which Jesus could have pointed in an attempt to illustrate blissful domestic life. Granted, the women come off slightly better than the men, but their virtue only serves to highlight the inadequacy of the marriages into which they entered.

Jesus and his own family

The group looking at this subject found little to go on.

Matthew's Gospel indicates that Joseph is a direct descendant of Abraham. That may buttress his value as the caretaker or step-father of Jesus, but it says little about his character. What we learn in the first chapter of Matthew's Gospel is that Joseph is so principled that he is keen to break off his engagement to Mary when he discovers that she is pregnant *(Matthew 1:19)*. But Joseph is also a man who, despite his high principles and moral standing, is open to illogical suggestions offered through the medium of dreams. In the first of these *(Matthew 1:20–22)* he is persuaded not to do the decent thing, but to do the exceptional thing and become the surrogate father to Mary's child.

Perhaps the decision was not totally based on supernatural persuasion. For if Joseph was aware of his ancestral lineage, he would have known that several of his named forebears were invited by God to do that which took them outside their comfort zone.

As regards Mary, we know virtually nothing of her pedigree. Though it is usually through the maternal lineage that a child is considered a true Jew, we do not know anything about Mary's parentage. The names traditionally given to her own mother and father are the stuff of legend rather than biblical witness, as are the presumptions that she was in her mid-teens when she became pregnant and always wore blue.

The more disconcerting thing for our purposes is that Jesus' life began in an awkward relationship: an unwed girl becoming pregnant and her fiancé, on discovering the news, being reluctant to go ahead with the marriage *(Matthew 1:18–20)*.

If the impoverished circumstances around his birth are not exceptional, his refugee status is something that not many people have shared *(Matthew 2:13–15)*.

But we do know that Jesus' relationship with his mother was far from that of doting parent and equally doting child. His absconding from the caravan of pilgrims returning home after the Passover shows Mary as someone beside herself with worry. When they find the twelve-year-old in the temple engaged in dialogue with people many times his age, it is Mary who articulates the upset felt by both parents, "Why have you treated us like this?" *(Luke 2:48b)*.

When he and his disciples are present at the wedding feast at Cana, where Mary seems to take precedence in the guest list *(John 2:1)*, there is a slight altercation behind Jesus' first demonstration of supernatural powers. The precise moment is when Mary says, "There's no wine left," and Jesus replies, "That is no concern of mine. My hour has not yet come" *(John 2:4b)*. Recently some scholars of John's Gospel have suggested that Jesus' rather severe retort to his mother could well be an expression of exasperation.

We see a further challenge to the sentimental notion of Jesus' relationship with Mary when news is brought to him that his family is outside the house in which he is speaking and would like to hear him. "Who is my mother? Who are my brothers?" he asks, before—as on other occasions—indicating that those who best assume that title are those who do God's will *(Matthew 12:46–50)*. Interestingly, he also indicates that it is not just in his own town that a prophet lacks honor, but also in his own family *(Matthew 13:57)*.

In a less immediate domestic setting, he is greeted by an admirer who shouts, "Happy the womb that carried you and the breasts that suckled you!" *(Luke 11:27b)*. To which Jesus more or less says, "No, that has nothing to do with it."

On two other occasions, it seems that his near family do not fully attest to his worth. In Galilee his "brothers" (a term that might refer to extended family) seem to doubt his judgment in keeping to the periphery when they encourage him to go public, "No one can hope for recognition if he works in obscurity ... Show yourself to the world." The immediate comment of the Gospel writer is rather telling: Even his brothers had no faith in him *(John 7:3–5)*.

The other instance is when, in equally direct terms, his family suggest that he is out of his mind *(Mark 3:21)*.

Now, granted, we are dealing with limited evidence. The Gospels are not a biography with insights into the intimate relationship between mother and son or among siblings. But what we have does not warrant the belief that Jesus modeled in himself ideal family life.

Sayings regarding family life

Surely there must be something in Jesus' teachings that sanctifies the family? That is what our third group of researchers had hoped. But again there were sparse pickings to fulfil their expectations. A few selected statements might suffice to undermine any notion that Jesus was a supporter of family values at all costs:

> Brother will hand over brother to death, and a father his child; children will turn against their parents and send them to their death. Everyone will hate you for your allegiance to me. *(Matthew 10:21–22)*

I have come not to bring peace to the earth ... but a sword. I have come to set a man against his father, a daughter against her mother, a daughter-in-law against her mother-in-law; and a man will find his enemies under his own roof. *(Matthew 10:34–36)*

No one is worthy of me who cares more for father or mother than for me; no one is worthy of me who cares more for son or daughter. *(Matthew 10:37)*

Truly I tell you: there is no one who has given up home, brothers or sisters, mother, father or children, or land, for my sake and for the gospel, who will not receive in this age a hundred times as much ... and persecutions besides; and in the age to come eternal life. *(Mark 10:29–30)*

Similar words appear in Luke's Gospel *(see Luke 9:59; 14:26; 21:16)*.

This is not to say that Jesus discourages family responsibility. He does, after all, ask the rich young man whether he keeps the commandment to honor his parents *(Luke 18:20)*. He warns against anything that might abuse children *(Mark 9:42)*, and he encourages the settling of inter-family squabbles by honest confrontation and forgiveness when guilt is regretted *(Luke 17:3)*.

He also clearly enjoys being in households—among others those of Joanna, Susanna, Lazarus and his sisters, and Peter. Though as some women from Lincoln Diocese pointed out to me a few years ago, while Peter's mother-in-law would be grateful to Jesus for healing her, she might want to give him a piece of her mind for taking the major breadwinner in the household away from his family and domestic responsibilities. Perhaps the father of James and John and the spouse of

Matthew (if he was married) might also have had a word to say about the domestic and economic disruption caused by devout discipleship.

But surely there's something yet more positive to be discovered? Does Jesus not make some salient comments about the sanctity of marriage? Doesn't he talk about the differences in the sexes being the reason for man and woman leaving their parents and becoming one flesh? Yes, he does. But, curiously, it is not in the context of advice dispensed to the disciples in case they have to lead a marital counseling course. His words on marriage come in the context of a question addressed to him about divorce.

We find evidence of that in Matthew's Gospel, beginnning at chapter 19, verse 3. It is a Pharisee—who may either be looking for greater leniency for divorce, or hoping to identify Jesus as a dangerous liberal—who asks if a man can divorce his wife "for any cause he pleases." Jesus here, as elsewhere *(e.g., Luke 16:18),* is quite unbending on divorce. It cannot happen on a male whim, but has to be because of proven adultery.

It is interesting that this is what is called a "dominical" instruction, a specific word on a moral issue from Jesus. He says nothing about relationships between people of the same sex, male or female. Yet this latter is the issue that vexes churches, while divorce has become a possibility even for Christian couples who simply don't get on with each other any longer.

Of stories that Jesus tells regarding families, the three principal ones hardly reflect patterns of a kind of domestic bliss to which people would aspire today. One parable is of a man in bed with his family who finds himself disturbed by a neighbor in the middle of the night *(Luke 11:5–8)*. The second has to do with the rather irregular wedding feast for a wealthy man's son in which beggars and rough sleepers are invited to the banquet *(Luke 14:12–24)*. And the third, the most famous of all, is of a dysfunctional family in which the father seems to exercise a degree of generosity of spirit beyond the tolerance level of most men *(Luke 15:11–24)*.

From the findings of all the innocent researchers on Iona, we do not discover substantial material to buttress the claim that Jesus initiated, espoused or encouraged what we now call "Christian Family Values." And that, perhaps, is for a reason that sometimes evades us; namely, at the time of Christ, families were nothing like the nuclear units we think of now.

Family life in first-century Palestine

In the previous chapter we noted how the majority of people, at the time of Jesus' ministry, were dead by the age of 30. The causes were mainly to do with disease, but the immediate effect was to make mother, father and 2.5 children the exception rather than the rule. It wasn't just older people who were confronted with untimely deaths, as the healings of Jairus' daughter, the widow of Nain's son, and the centurion's servant indicate. But the premature death of adults, whether male or female, would inevitably leave a family without a father or a mother. Indeed, perhaps in thinking of the first century, we should see one-parent families as the norm rather than the exception because of the high death rate.

In this situation, the ministry of Jesus was concerned with initiating a unit of belonging in which, to put it theologically, water is thicker than blood. For Jesus, the pedigree of a person was not the defining issue. Those who were allied to him, as ultimately signified by baptism, entered not just into a personal relationship with their Savior, but into a family relationship with all the others gathered into his church.

Here, in what Malina and Rohrbaugh call the "fictive kin group," people are intended to find security, belonging and identity, which will sustain them should their own biological family die or denounce them.

This is the radical identity, which most churches have hardly glimpsed. It is not Jesus spiriting people away from their own homes in the manner of the Moonies or the Children of God. Rather, it is Jesus inviting people into a larger family that is defined by commitment to the Kingdom of God rather than bondage to ancestral tradition.

It is the kind of belonging that I saw in Guguletu, a suburb of Cape Town. There the J. L. Zwane Church takes seriously the reality of a community riddled with HIV. One in four people are positive. There is a wide range of ministries that serve the needs and affirm the potentials of sufferers and carers alike. But there are also some more private forms of caring. When I visited the church in 2005, I was introduced to a woman in her fifties, an unmarried lady who had never had any children. But because so many of the mothering and fathering age group were dying, she decided that, within the body of Christ, she could not absent herself from sharing responsibility for the community, so she took to her home four orphaned boys. Was there ever a better example of the verse that ends Psalm 113:

[God] makes the woman in a childless house
a happy mother of children. *(Psalm 113:9)*

However, I do not believe that Jesus initiated the Christian community merely to deal with the casualties of a society with a high death rate. I believe there are two deeper reasons for encouraging this trans-biological bonding.

The first is enshrined in a proverb variously attributed to China, Africa and John Wesley, namely that "it takes a village to rear a child." No biological family is sufficient. Indeed some biological families may be stifling for the full development of children and parents alike. We are not Russian dolls that fit into each other. We are, in every family, people of different attributes and attitudes. Wives cannot be totally sustained by the companionship of their husbands; they need the company of others. Boys, especially during the rebellious adolescent years, need adults other than their parents to confide in and learn from.

The encouragement that we receive from other people of faith should be a means by which our horizons are extended and the potentials unrecognized by our biological family are identified and affirmed.

I believe also that Jesus saw the church as a surrogate community because neither marriage nor family life can be mandatory for everyone. Jesus himself said that there were some people for whom marriage was not an option *(Matthew 19:11)*. Does that mean that single people, and widows and orphans, and divorcees should be denied the close companionship of others?

Do children, who have been battered by a sadist of a father, have no recourse to a better role model that they might emulate when they become parents themselves? Do the husband and wife who, despite prayer and medical treatment, find themselves unable to conceive have forever to feel outsiders to "normal" society, particularly where churches use Mothering Sunday as a time to praise fertile women rather than rejoice in the mothering that God and God's church offers to all?

Two surrogate family scenarios

I have a friend in heaven whose name is Gabi de Wil. She spent all of her life in Belgium, and much of it as a member of the parish of the Beguinage in Brussels. Into that church, one Saturday at the time of the afternoon Mass, wandered a young man called Jean Claude. No one knew him, but people welcomed him.

He returned week after week, and was evidently glad to be in that community, among whom one of the friends he made was Gabi. In time he revealed to a few people something of his story, namely that he had been thrown out of his home by his parents when he told them he was gay, that he had slept rough in the streets, and that he now lived in a hostel.

In due course, Jean Claude asked if he might be confirmed in the faith, and that happened at the Easter Vigil. Some time later, he confided to Gabi that he had discovered he was HIV positive—at a time when there were no antiretrovirals to combat the disease.

Eventually, when he became very ill, he was admitted to a hospice, to which Gabi would go regularly to visit the boy, sing to him, pray with him and make him laugh with her outrageous stories. When he died, many of the parish attended his funeral. But as mourners left the graveside, Gabi saw one woman remaining who was not from the church. She approached her and asked if she was, by any chance, Jean Claude's mother. She replied in the affirmative.

"Madame," said Gabi, "I want to tell you two things: that your son died a peaceful death, and that he died as a Christian."

What or who was it who enabled him to die in this way? Jean Claude was about 21 when he died. Gabi de Wil was almost four times his age. Yet she had been for him a surrogate mother, aunt and girlfriend, representing the family of Jesus in which water is thicker than blood.

The other scenario is much better known. It is, in fact, the moment at which we might recognize how this new unit of belonging was initiated by Jesus. It is at the cross as he, the dying Savior, looks at those standing around, and turns the attention of the faithful, yet grief-stricken, Mary to a young man close by, saying, "Mother, there is your son." And to the young man, "Son, there is your mother." Ever since, those who belong to Jesus have had to see themselves as also belonging to each other.

Chapter five

The religious reprobate

Faith and conflict

In what became one of the most contentious religious books of the twentieth century, the Anglican Bishop of Woolwich, John Robinson, initiated a season of religious controversy, which took over the front pages of even the popular press.

What Robinson essentially did in *Honest to God* was to make accessible to the wider public theological thinking, which was at that time decades old. Some saw it as the thin end of a dangerously libertarian wedge that threatened the integrity of the Christian faith. Revisiting that book (first published in the 1960s), today, one wonders what all the fuss was about.

Yet in *Honest to God*, as in many of his other books, Robinson sometimes offers an illustration that clearly exemplifies one or other of the eternal dilemmas involved in the life of faith.

One such is of the convergence of two processions on Good Friday. The first is a traditional march of witness such as many Anglican parish churches might hold during Holy Week. The other is a protest march against Britain's possession and potential use of nuclear weapons. Robinson poses the question as to which of these two should win the sympathy of the Christian—that which bears witness to the Savior of the world, or that which indicates the continuing need of the world to be saved.

Such a dilemma must often have been in the heart of Jesus as he found himself continually in conflict with the religious establishment (to which he subscribed) as it seemed so at odds with the intentions of the Kingdom of God (which he came to proclaim).

The home-church sermon

This can be seen clearly in his first appearance in his home synagogue. Luke offers a detailed account of the event *(see Luke 4:14–30).*

At first the congregation admire his erudition as he reads from the scroll that contains the word of the prophet Isaiah:

The spirit of the Lord is upon me
because he has anointed me.

This passage is associated with the Jubilee, the event every fifty years when the Jews were meant to forgive debts, liberate captives, and reconcile themselves to each other and to the purposes of God.

Jesus, however, sees this as the mandate for his recently begun public ministry and announces that "today"—not some time twenty or thirty years in the future—on that very day on which he reads of God's holistic liberation of the world and its people, this same event is initiated.

Whether it is this pronouncement, or his allusions to Jewish history (which we will consider later), the home crowd are not well pleased. They turn quickly from admiring his elocution to despising his presence. This is not simply a matter of muffled noises of dissent. They rise up, eject him from the synagogue and take him to the brow of the hill on which the town is built, not so that together they might admire the view, but so that he might be thrown to his death.

Where does his loyalty lie? With the institution of religion that has formed him, cradled the scriptures, nurtured generations of teachers and scholars, and wishes to remain unshaken? Or is he called to speak to and for those who are usually absent from the palaces of religion, whose experience of life is more of social injustice than spiritual security? Does he come to celebrate the usual feasts or to initiate the long-term movement, which will eventually culminate in the judgment of the earth's nations and the satisfaction of human longings at the wedding feast of the Lamb in heaven?

It is within religious precincts that Jesus is constantly scrutinized, criticized and threatened. And yet he does not exempt himself from engaging with worshipping communities.

A prophecy of dissension

The ambivalent relationship between Jesus and his faith community is something we find first alluded to in the infancy stories of Luke's Gospel. When Mary and Joseph take the infant Jesus to the Jerusalem temple for a dedication ceremony, they are met by a veteran believer called Simeon who has been waiting for a sign from God that his nation would be restored. He recognizes that the child Jesus is the sign.

Many people will be familiar with Simeon's words, which are enshrined in the canticle known as the *Nunc Dimittis*. Its most familiar English translation, taken from the King James Version, begins:

> Lord, now lettest thou thy servant depart in peace. ...
> For mine eyes have seen thy salvation. *(Luke 2:29–30)*

Less popular are the lines of prophetic insight that Simeon says to Mary after blessing the hitherto happy parents:

> This child is destined to be a sign that will be rejected; and you too will be pierced to the heart. Many in Israel will stand or fall because of him; and so the secret thoughts of many will be laid bare. *(Luke 2:34–35)*

Prophetic words indeed, for they adequately describe the mixture of hope and consternation that followed the words and actions of Jesus whenever he was in religious precincts. For Jesus regarded the synagogues and temple as venues in which he could legitimately speak of God's kingdom. On several occasions the Gospels indicate this activity in general— "Jesus went round . . . teaching in their synagogues" *(Matthew 9:35)*—but specific venues are also mentioned: Capernaum *(Mark 1:21)*, Galilee *(Matthew 4:23)*, Judaea *(Luke 4:44)* and Nazareth *(Luke 4:16)*.

Teaching, one of the responsibilities of being a rabbi, was one of three activities in which Jesus participated when in religious precincts. The other two were preaching and healing. It is rather difficult to distinguish, from the Gospel records, what precisely differentiated teaching and preaching. For, apart from the aforementioned episode in his home synagogue, we have little evidence of what he specifically said in such settings. Maybe teaching and preaching were combined.

The sermon reviewed

Certainly Luke indicates that when Jesus visited his home synagogue there was both proclamation and exegesis. The proclamation was that the day of deliverance had dawned. That was what delighted people. The exegesis consisted in nothing more than making two allusions to recorded Jewish history in which God did not opt in favor of those who believed themselves to be chosen.

The instances would be known to his listening congregation. The first referred to how Elijah, during a time of famine, favored not a Jewish but a Sidonian widow with a visit that guaranteed her a constant food supply *(1 Kings 17:9–16)*. The second anecdote was from the life of Elisha, Elijah's protégé. At a time when many people in Israel suffered from leprosy, Elisha was guided by God to restore the health of Naaman, who was a Syrian *(2 Kings 5:1–14)*.

With these two biblical illustrations, Jesus indicated and celebrated the breadth of God's compassion, which is for the world, not for a select few; and he used the illustrations as proof texts to demonstrate how "no prophet is recognized in his own country."

This is what turned an admiring crowd into an angry mob that, in dragging Jesus to the hill on which the town was built with the intention of throwing him over the cliff, unwittingly illustrated what he had just alluded to.

The truth of the good old days

There is always something disturbing about being reminded of one's full rather than partial religious pedigree. In Scotland—as elsewhere in Britain—the year 2007 bore witness to that.

As a Glaswegian, I had always believed that Britain's engagement in the slave trade was a predominantly English affair. I had been to Bristol and seen the still-named White

Ladies' Walk and Black Boy Hill. But in 2007, the year celebrating the passing of a bill in the Westminster parliament to end slavery within the British Empire, the publication of a book called *Scotland and the Slave Trade* by Iain Whyte opened windows on a forgotten part of our history.

I had in ignorance imagined that the Jamaica Bridge in Glasgow was a local allusion to a fond colony. I was unaware that 45 percent of the slave plantations in that country were owned by Scots. Nor was I aware that St. Vincent Street, which runs through the city, was not a condescending gesture by the Protestant city council to the minority Catholic population, but again was indicative of Scottish engagement in slavery affecting that Caribbean island. And it was Christian traders and Christian churches who enabled and endorsed this practice of human degradation.

For long it was imagined that the slave-ship captain John Newton, the author of the text "Amazing Grace," had penned the words after becoming an abolitionist. Not at all. His evangelical faith encouraged him to hold services on deck for the crew, but there was no attempt to enable the emancipation of the slaves who endured the brutality of a transatlantic crossing in chains below deck.

Perhaps more singularly for us in Scotland, there was a period in the nineteenth century known as the "Clearances" when absentee landlords sent lowland managers into highland regions to evict peasant farmers who had tilled the soil for generations in order that sheep might safely graze in their stead. This chapter of history, long unvisited by successive generations of clergy, stands for ever as an indictment of religious leaders who separate faith from justice. For with the promise of larger stipends and improved lodgings, the

Presbyterian clergy were encouraged to rub salt in the wounds of those being evicted by preaching that this forced expatriation was intended by God as a punishment for their sins.

There are moments in all our collective pasts that we do not like to have reinvoked, either because they bear witness to our flawed natures or—as in the case of the sermon at Nazareth—they point to a God who is not the patron saint of those who wield the power.

Controversial healing

But perhaps more controversial than what Jesus said within religious precincts is what he did. He was the great troubler of the defenders of the faith, for whenever he was present things changed. And for those who believed that God and change did not inhabit the same space, the appearance of Jesus in the local synagogue or national temple was not good news.

We tend to identify evidence of that from his last visit to the temple, when he upset trade in the name of justice, for indeed those who were exchanging money and selling sacrificial animals were not so much aiding devotion as effectively preventing poorer people and foreigners from worshipping.

Regarding this particular occasion, it is interesting to note what is frequently forgotten, namely that his turning over of the tables was not the activity that produced the most vitriolic response. It was two other activities. Here is the full story, as recorded by St. Matthew *(Matthew 21:12–17)*.

> Jesus went into the temple and drove out all who were buying and selling in the temple precincts; he upset

the tables of the money-changers and the seats of the dealers in pigeons, and said to them, "Scripture says, 'My house shall be called a house of prayer'; but you are making it a bandits' cave."

In the temple the blind and the crippled came to him, and he healed them. When the chief priests and scribes saw the wonderful things he did, and heard the boys in the temple shouting, "Hosanna to the Son of David!" they were indignant and asked him, "Do you hear what they are saying?" Jesus answered, "I do. Have you never read the text, 'You have made children and babes at the breast sound your praise aloud'?" Then he left them and went out of the city to Bethany, where he spent the night.

John's Gospel, which sets this story towards the beginning of Jesus' ministry, covers the first incident only *(John 2:13– 22)* and, as with Matthew, there is no mention of a violent reaction from the tradespeople to whom he quotes scripture as a warrant for his actions.

What incurs evident displeasure is his admiration for the untutored voices of children whose song echoes what they or their parents may have been shouting on the day Jesus rode into Jerusalem.

It would be disingenuous (though tempting to some) to build, on the basis of this singular event, a theology of the place of children in worship. More easily justified would be the claim that in these three activities—disrupting trade, enjoying the song of children, and healing the sick—Jesus deliberately demonstrated his intention that the place of worship should be wholly inclusive and that economic status, age or infirmity should not be made barriers to participation in the worshipping community.

But it is the healing in the temple that deserves a little more comment. For it is completely consonant with what Jesus has done previously in religious precincts.

Here is the Gospel record:

Mark 1:39 He traveled through Galilee, preaching in synagogues and driving out demons.

Mark 3:1–6 He went into a synagogue where there was a man with a withered arm and he cured him.

Luke 4:31–37 In Capernaum he went into a synagogue and healed a man who was possessed by a demon.

Luke 13:10–17 While teaching in a synagogue he cured a woman who had been bent double for 18 years.

To these, add three other incidents that relate to synagogue life: the healing of the daughter of Jairus, who was the president of a synagogue *(Luke 8:49–56)*; his instruction to a single leper whom he had cured to go and show himself to the priest *(Luke 5:12–16)*; and a similar instruction to ten men similarly diseased *(Luke 17:11–18)*.

For Jesus, the place of prayer is, evidently, also the place of healing. But that was not something that his co-religionists always appreciated.

When he heals the man with the withered arm, "the Pharisees, on leaving the synagogue, at once began plotting with the men of Herod's party to bring about Jesus' death" *(Mark 3:6)*. This extreme reaction in a synagogue is paralleled in the temple on a number of occasions. One is when, after Jesus accused the merchants of turning the house of prayer for all nations into a robber's cave, "the chief priests and the scribes heard of this and looked for a way to bring about his death." Others can be found in John 7 and 8, where we read of the crowd asking,

"Is not this the man they want to put to death?" *(John 7:25)*. Later we read that in response to Jesus' words "they tried to seize him" *(John 7:30)*. Soon after, "The Pharisees overheard these mutterings about him among the people, so [they] sent temple police to arrest him" *(John 7:32)*.

A day or two later we discover that after Jesus referred to himself (as elsewhere) as being water from which people could drink, "Some were for arresting him, but no one laid hands on him" *(John 7:44)*. And later yet, when speaking near the temple treasury and using another favorite metaphor to describe himself, that of being the light of the world, "no one arrested him, because his hour had not yet come" *(John 8:20)*.

When he cured the crippled woman in a synagogue, "his opponents were covered with confusion, while the mass of the people were delighted at all the wonderful things he was doing" *(Luke 13:17)*. And that confusion would certainly have been felt by the priests who had to reincorporate into the community lepers whom they previously would have ceremonially banished *(Luke 17:14)*.

Holistic faith never easy

We must conclude that although Jesus' relationship to the citadels of religion seems ambivalent, it is actually grounded in integrity. He believed in attending public worship, and he frequently took a role of leadership, which endeared him to some people and alienated others. He also clearly indicated that he was not prepared to redeem souls while leaving minds, bodies and economic systems unchanged. His miracles in religious precincts and his challenge to corrupt practices were indicative of an understanding of faith in which the whole of our being—spiritual, moral, intellectual, economic—has to be laid open to the gracious amendment of God. Anything less is a partial faith for disintegrated people.

But the fact that the public ministry of Jesus in teaching, preaching and healing in synagogue and temple should result in attempts to ensure his assassination is a sober reminder of how people of religious faith are as prone to defying God as any others. For when sacrosanct customs, conventional respectability and exclusive communities are shown as defective in the light of the gospel, our fondness for what has shaped us has to be made subservient to the summons of the one who alone can redeem us.

Chapter six

Feminine faces

An innocent exercise

I should have known that something was amiss when one side of the room looked puzzled and the other was animated.

It was at a conference center in Regina, Saskatchewan. Some people had been at the event at which I had just finished working and were staying on for a day or two. Others had arrived early for the next week's event. There would be around sixty people and I had been asked if I would lead morning worship and do something "interactive."

Given that there were children as well as adults, I decided on a participative Bible study. I read selected verses from the Gospel alluding to Jesus' male disciples and the women who followed him, but never mentioned specific names.

I then asked the company to divide in two. One half were to go into smaller groups and, without recourse to the Bible, remember the twelve male disciples, write their names on large pieces of paper and note beside each three things we knew about the disciples.

The other side of the room had to do the same, but with women in mind. Acknowledging that not every woman who followed Jesus was named, and that a good few were called Mary (there must have been a shortage of girls' names in those days!), people in these small groups might have to find other ways of identifying the women concerned.

Both sides of the room had twenty minutes each, but the first set of groups were stumped long before then.

What do you call them?

These were the people who were trying to remember the men who are depicted in glass and sometimes in statue in almost every cathedral, the men after whom hundreds of thousands of churches are named. Nobody, it seemed, could remember the twelve disciples.

The likely suspects were commonly agreed to be Peter, James and John ... then Andrew ... Matthew ... Judas ... Thomas ... Philip ... And then people got stuck. What about the other four?

They are James the Less—or James, son of Alphaeus—Thaddeus, Simon the Zealot ... and, of course, Bartholomew. Except in Luke's Gospel where there is no Thaddeus, but there is Judas, son of James. And then, of course, John confuses things by bringing in somebody called Nathaniel ...

Be that as it may, when people tried to write three things generally known about these founding fathers of the church, it was far from easy.

We know plenty about Peter and a little about Judas, and several things about John the "beloved disciple." But what about the rest?

To Jesus, Andrew brought Peter; a little boy with loaves and fishes; and some Greeks ... for which he is the patron saint of Scotland.

Matthew we remember as a tax-collector and probable author. We know that Thomas' major contribution to the

Gospels was evidence of a doubting mind. We know that Philip brought Nathaniel to Jesus, was asked a question about fast food by Jesus, and baptized an Ethiopian eunuch ... and not much more.

But what about James the Less? Simon the Zealot? Thaddeus or Jude or Bartholomew?

Substantial women

By contrast, the people recounting the women who followed Jesus were having a field day.

They discovered quite a lot about Mary, apart from the presumption that she wore a blue gown and never looked pregnant.

They discovered—to my great surprise—that the Woman at the Well was the only person in the Gospels to whom a whole chapter is devoted to cover her encounter with Jesus. And no wonder. Andrew brings a few Greeks to Jesus, but this woman brings a whole village *(John 4:27–30)*. Why has no nation chosen her as patron saint?

They discovered that Mary and Martha were an interesting pair. On one occasion, while Martha seemed to ignore what Jesus was saying, Mary sat attentively at his feet *(Luke 10:39–42)*. But Martha the housewife was actually multi-tasking. For when Lazarus their brother died, she was the one who expressed the faith that Jesus could raise him. It was the more pious Mary who expressed doubt *(John 11:21–32)*.

Together we discovered that the woman in Luke's Gospel who washed Jesus' feet with her tears and anointed them with precious ointment *(Luke 7:37–38)* had more verses covering her specific activity than had eight of the male disciples. The same comparable coverage is also true for the Syro-Phoenician woman who has the rare accolade of being the only person in the Gospels who seems to have got Jesus to change his mind *(Mark 7:27–29)*.

And then there were the other women who followed him … like Joanna and Susanna who provided food and lodging for Jesus and his slightly anonymous merry men *(Luke 8:3)*. And three or four women, most of them called Mary, who (unlike the male disciples) were present for Jesus' burial *(Matthew 27:55–56)*, as is true of Mary of Magdala, the first witness to the resurrection.

Perhaps it would be good to list all the women associated with Jesus, acknowledging that not all of them could be said to have followed him.

- Elizabeth, cousin of Mary, who blessed the fruit of her womb/*Luke 1:42*
- Mary, mother of Jesus/*Luke 1:38*
- Anna, an 84-year-old prophetess, who recognized Jesus as liberator/*Luke 2:36*
- Simon Peter's mother-in-law whom he heals/*Mark 1:30*
- A Samaritan woman he meets at a well/*John 4:7*
- A woman caught committing adultery/*John 8:3*
- The widow of Nain whose son he brings back to life/ *Luke 7:11*
- A woman of immoral reputation who washes his feet with tears/*Luke 7:37*
- The hemorrhaging woman whom he heals/*Mark 5:25*
- Jairus' daughter whom he heals/*Mark 5:35*

- The Syro-Phoenician woman who argues with him/ *Mark 7:25*
- A "number of women"/*Luke 8:2*
- Mary of Magdala whom he healed and who met the resurrected Jesus/*Luke 8:2 & John 20:16*
- Joanna, the wife of Chuza (one of Herod's stewards)/ *Luke 8:2*
- Susanna, friend of Joanna, with whom she provided food and lodging/*Luke 8:2*
- Martha, into whose house he enters/*Luke 10:38*
- Mary, sister of Martha and Lazarus, who also anointed him/*Luke 10:39 & John 11:2*
- A woman who calls out to him words of encouragement/ *Luke 11:27*
- Women called his "sisters"/*Mark 6:3*
- A woman bent double for eighteen years whom he heals and names "a daughter of Abraham"/*Luke 13:16*
- The wife of Pilate who is troubled about Jesus' trial/ *Matthew 27:19*
- Women who wept as Jesus walked to Calvary/*Luke 23:27*
- Mary, the mother of James and Joseph, present at the crucifixion/*Matthew 27:56*
- The wife of Zebedee, present at the crucifixion/ *Matthew 27:56*
- Salome who was present at the crucifixion/*Mark 15:40*

Here are over twenty women who in one way or another were admirers or followers of Jesus. I never anticipated this number would be so great. Somehow the teaching of the church has stressed discipleship as a primarily male activity, modeled by men. But, if we look closer, we may discover some equally surprising things:

a. *Jesus never gives a woman a telling off or speaks to her as an inferior.*

Contrast that to the way he gives ripostes to Peter, saying to him on one occasion, "Out of my sight, Satan; you are a stumbling block to me" *(Matthew 16:23)*. But the other eleven are included when Jesus, on more than one occasion, asks the rhetorical questions: How long do I have to put up with you? Where is your faith?

It is men whom he chastises for trying to keep children away from him, and it is men who are the subject and object of his teaching when he indicates that adultery is as present in contemplating the prospect as committing the offense.

b. *It is in women, more than men, that he finds models of faithful living.*

On two occasions he says that he has "never seen such faith in all Israel." One occasion is when the centurion says that he believes Jesus can heal his servant without seeing him *(Matthew 8:5–10)*; the other is when he has the disputatious meeting with the Canaanite woman whose daughter is ill *(Matthew 15:21–28)*. Elsewhere, those who demonstrate faith are frequently foreigners.

Only once does he single out someone as a model for generosity, and that is the poor widow who drops two copper coins into the offering bowl *(Mark 12:41–44)*. When he is looking for a model of genuine prayer it is the laconic humility of a tax collector and the persistence of a widow *(Luke 18:1–14)* that he extols— both of whom were peripheral to regular religious society.

And on the only occasion when he makes a recorded comment on gracious hospitality, it is not the Pharisee who is hosting him at a meal in his house whom he commends, but a female interloper who washes his feet with her tears *(Luke 7:36–50)*.

c. Jesus takes illustrations from women's experience.

Unlike many male orators and preachers throughout the ages who focus mainly on illustrations from the experience of men, and only occasionally allude to the world of women, Jesus has no difficulty in taking examples from the woman's world, and sometimes he provides parallel illustrations.

	Male	*Female*
Matthew 9:16–17	Old wineskins for old wine	Old patches for old garments
Matthew 13:31–33	A man sows mustard seed	A woman takes yeast
Luke 15:4–10	A shepherd seeks a lost lamb	A woman looks for a lost coin

In light of the last example, it seems odd that we have no difficulty in thinking of or physically depicting God as the Shepherd who brings back the lost lamb, but seldom do we think of God as the woman who goes down on her knees to find the lost coin.

d. Jesus' compassion for women is often contrasted with the disdain of other men.

Whenever Jesus extols or has compassion for a woman, there are always males in the background who are appalled, some because the virtue or penitence evident in the woman is in marked contrast to its absence in the men. Here are some examples:

John 8:1–11   Woman caught in adultery
vs. her captors

79

John 4:1–42	Woman at the well vs. disgusted disciples
Luke 7:36–42	First anointing woman vs. Pharisee host
Mark 12:41–44	Poor widow vs. disregarding rich men
Matthew 26:6–13	Second anointing woman vs. the disciples
Mark 10:13–15	Women with children vs. men keeping them away
Luke 13:10–17	Crippled woman vs. synagogue dignitaries

By contrast, when Jesus extols or expresses compassion for a man, there is no band of harpies registering their complaint.

In this ability to affirm women, to use their life experiences as substance for his parables, in his clear ability to be comfortable with women around him and to enable them to be comfortable in his presence, Jesus is not only singular for his time, but also at odds with many Christian men today.

A few years ago I was working in a rich neighborhood, where one of the engagements involved speaking at a prayer breakfast attended by around two hundred people at 6:30 in the morning. The great novelty was that this was being cooked by the men of the church, some of whom let it be known that they had been there since 3 o'clock ... (which perhaps accounts for the sausages being so hard. I'm sure women could have done it with greater aplomb starting two hours later.)

Apart from the forced bravado, back-slapping and camaraderie that the men exhibited on this singular occasion, I was taken aback when the man in charge asked one of the women present to say grace, after which he commented:

I think that she did that so well, we'll have to ask her back another time.

Jesus would not have been so patronizing. Perhaps, had he been around today, he would have been keen to draw attention to statistics that have probably remained much the same since his earthly ministry:

Women make up half the world's population,
do two-thirds of the world's productive work,
own ten percent of the world's wealth,
and one percent of the world's land.

Unlike many men, Jesus was in tune with and unashamed of his feminine side. It was not a shadow self. It was an essential part of his being that, in a society biased to the masculine, enabled him to enter into extraordinary empathy with women, particularly those who were vulnerable, such as the women with children for whom he feared coming persecution *(Luke 23:28–29)*.

But there was something else about his intuition and use of language that evaded me until I ended up staying at a seminary in Manila in the Philippines.

The seminary was next to a river that, when flooded, rose by five feet. The bamboo houses in which the staff lived were therefore on stilts. My visit was in the dry season, so under the house was a dry river bed with nets spread out to catch falling leaves and prevent them from choking the drains.

There were chickens in the vicinity, and while I was aware that the roosters liked to awaken the dawn, I had no idea that these infernal creatures would start their serenade at half past three.

One morning things were even noisier. Two of the cockerels started fighting each other and landed in the nets under one of the nearby houses. There the birds created mayhem, stemming from their shared experience of animosity and entanglement. Eventually some kind soul got up and removed the offending creatures from the nets.

It was then that I realized how, when Jesus looked with compassion on the people of Jerusalem *(Matthew 23:37)*, he could never have said,

> How I long to gather you under my wings like a *rooster* gathers *his* chickens.

A masculine illustration would have been futile. The female witness was indispensable.

Chapter seven

Talking to strangers

Viva Mexico

I was giving a series of talks in a very affluent part of North Carolina, dealing with aspects of Christ's ministry not usually discussed in church. Much of the content is included below. But it is the sequel with which I want to begin.

The morning after one particular lecture, the pastor of the church, a delightful and caring man, mentioned without accusation that the talk the previous evening might have been difficult for the congregation to listen to.

"How come?" I asked. And he replied, "Because of the Mexicans." "But I didn't see any in church," I responded. "No," he said, "there weren't any there. But there are quite a lot in the vicinity. The thing is that people are quite glad to have them as gardeners or domestic helps, but they don't want them to live here. And there are now several in a settlement near the fringes of the town."

That afternoon, I happened to go into the local Roman Catholic church to pray and enjoy its quietness. During the half hour I was in, three Mexican workers, independent of each other, came into the church, genuflected, then knelt to pray—or in one case lay prostrate—in front of the altar. I pondered the question within myself: what's up with these Presbyterians that they can't see the faith in people of a different culture in the way that Jesus did?

For that is indeed what Jesus did. His life was one that engaged him with people who did not necessarily share either his faith, or his culture or nationality.

Jesus' early experiences with foreigners

At the beginning and close of Jesus' life are foreign bookends. Matthew, in the story we read at Epiphany, tells of wise men or Magi who come from the East in order to find the one whom they believe to be "the new-born king of the Jews" *(Matthew 2:2)*. Where exactly they came from we do not know, but a frequent conjecture is Mesopotamia, later known as Persia and presently known as Iraq. If that were the case, it would be magnificent poetry, because on the way to Calvary Jesus is aided in carrying the cross by an African who is press-ganged into his service. His name is Simon and he comes from the region then called Cyrene, now referred to as Libya. So, appositely for a time when much of the world is engaged in an alleged "War on Terror," we find that Jesus was positively associated with people who came from areas recently branded as members of the "Axis of Evil."

But, of course, that was not the only occasion on which Jesus had been helped by people from the continent of Africa. Matthew, who tells us about the Magi, also informs us that Jesus had to flee the country soon after their visit. Herod, who feared a rival monarch, decided to cull all boys aged two and under *(Matthew 2:16)*. We have no idea how long this episode lasted. What we do know is that by the age of eleven at the latest Jesus was living in the town of Nazareth with his parents *(Luke 2:39)*.

It would be wrong to speculate as to what the experience of living in exile may have meant for someone so young. Its significance would probably be related through the years by his parents. But it might be sufficient for our purposes to recognize that here we have the Son of God experiencing a state similar to that known by refugees and asylum-seekers—aliens in a land not their own, among people of a different language, with no security of tenure. Perhaps it was the hospitality shown to Jesus and his family in the alien land that made him keen to be accommodating to people of different ethnic and religious backgrounds throughout his ministry.

Precedents in Hebrew scriptures

In receiving gifts from foreigners or perceiving in them qualities consonant with the kingdom of heaven, Jesus continually created uneasiness among his co-religionists. We have already noted some things above, which need not be repeated at length here, particularly the upset Jesus caused in his home synagogue by alluding to two moments in the biblical records where first Elijah and later Elisha showed kindness to people who were not Jews *(Luke 4:21–30)*.

These prophetic figures stood against the smugness of a community of people who believed that because they once had been deemed "chosen" and had a long history of favor from God, they could presume that an ever-benign Providence was on their side, allowing them to be dismissive and even hateful of others.

The Hebrew scriptures recount incidents and indicate legislation that people of faith find awkward to read. And there seem to be inherent contradictions. In one place we find laws discouraging inter-racial marriage, but then we look at Jesus' genealogy and discover that the four women mentioned were not born Hebrew. In some places we find the Israelites warring against the surrounding tribes; at other moments they enter into covenants with them.

Was it ever different in the long history of any nation? One just has to look at the curious allegiances among countries such as England, Scotland, France and Germany in post-Reformation times to see that a nation's friend can become its foe in less than a century.

Among the ancient Hebrews, there were always people on the prophetic wing who believed that God was *not* a tribal chieftain residing in a distant heaven.

Where Elijah and Elisha had—in God's name—shown favor to foreigners, Jeremiah was imprisoned for daring to suggest that the army currently laying siege to Jerusalem had God on its side and that struggling against it was futile *(Jeremiah 32:1–5)*.

Amos the Israelite looks out on regions neighboring the lands of his own people and one by one pronounces judgment on them. Damascus, Gaza, Tyre, Edom and others are systematically criticized and damned. Then he turns to Judah and Israel, the nations whom God has chosen. But rather than pat them on the back and remind them of their privileged status, he indicts them every bit as ferociously as he did the others *(Amos 1 & 2)*.

On a more positive note, Isaiah breaks through the tribalism of the times and offers a vision not of a future day when all in Israel will be reconciled with God, but of a great banquet on a high mountain provided by God for people of all nations *(Isaiah 25:6–8)*. This interplay between the favoring of the chosen people and evidence of greater magnanimity of the Divine Spirit is a constant in the Psalms: there are verses that curse the one-time enemy *(Psalm 137)* and other passages that anticipate that somehow Jerusalem and the people of Israel will be a unifying force enabling all nations to worship God *(Psalms 67 & 100)*.

A universal mission

It is this universal aspect of Israel's mission that is announced by Mary in the Magnificat, where she anticipates that *"all* generations will count me blessed" *(Luke 1:48)*, and by Simeon who sees the Christ child as the one who is "a light [to] bring revelation to the Gentiles" *(Luke 2:32)*. Later Jesus himself, quoting an ancient source, reminds his audience that the temple is to be "a house of prayer for all nations" *(Mark 11:17)*. The same intention is reflected in the words of commission to the disciples that conclude Matthew's Gospel:

Go therefore to all nations. *(Matthew 28:19)*

However, in the ministry of Jesus, engagement with and an admiration for people from different ethnic backgrounds is specific rather than general. Samaritans seem to have a particular significance for him. That nation provides both the character who has the longest recorded exchange with Jesus and the hero of arguably his most famous parable.

A first lady

The encounter with the woman at the well takes up nearly all of chapter four in John's Gospel. The nature of the exchange she has with Jesus is dependent on how we depict her. Is she a guilt-ridden wretch, a woman abused and rejected because she is infertile, or someone who, as the Americans say, "has been round the block a few times"?

My own image of her changed when I attended Mass in St Augustine's Roman Catholic Church in Washington DC. It is an all-Black congregation, with a great musical and preaching tradition. After the processional hymn, the pastor introduced the Mass with an unusual allusion to the Gospel, which may be roughly transcribed thus:

> We're here today because we worship a God whose name is love. Amen?
> AMEN!
> We're here today because we worship a God who loves each of us as if there were only one to love. Amen?
> AMEN
> We're here today because we worship a God who even loves women who've had five husbands. Amen???
> (THE CONGREGATION SHRIEKS WITH LAUGHTER)

There are so many unusual aspects to the story, some explicit, some implicit.

Jesus, a Jewish rabbi, is clearly visible in a Gentile location such as most of his fellow rabbis would avoid, and is engaged in intimate conversation with a woman whose marital history would discredit him. We know this both from historical background and from the recorded fact that when the disciples, who were off finding lunch, returned they were "astonished to find him talking with a woman" *(John 4:27)*. Even their attempts to distract him with food are met with a rebuff. He is evidently enjoying the conversation, which ends with the woman going away to round up a crowd of her fellow Samaritans to meet Jesus. She—the woman at the well—is effectively the first evangelist, whose success is not in converting others but in leading them to Jesus who enables conversion within them *(John 4:41–42)*.

This is the only instance where a crowd of people, from a race to which the Jews were hostile, enters into close contact with Jesus. Although admittedly he does rub shoulders with smaller numbers of foreigners, as when Andrew and Philip seek him out to tell him that there are some Greeks who would like to meet him *(John 12:20–22)*.

Three favored foreigners

Returning to individuals, we might note three of varied Gentile stock whom Jesus particularly appreciates.

The first is the grateful leper. One of ten, the rest presumably being Jewish, he alone returns to thank Jesus for effecting his cure. Does he do this because, as a non-Jew, he has no need to show himself to the priest like the others, or is it that he recognizes in Jesus the fount of real rather than routine religion? We don't know, but we do know that on seeing him come back, Jesus expresses both admiration and amazement:

> Were not all ten made clean? The other nine, where are they? Was no one found returning to give praise to God except this foreigner? *(Luke 17:17–18)*

The second non-Jew whom Jesus especially values is the woman referred to as Syro-Phoenician *(Mark 7:26)* or Canaanite *(Matthew 15:21)*. Most people would today refer to her as being Syrian (another constituent member of the Axis of Evil). She has a daughter who is ill and wants Jesus to heal the child. The ensuing conversation has been interpreted in a number of ways, particularly the phrase Jesus uses when he says that it is wrong to take the children's bread and throw it to the dogs *(Matthew 15:22)*. Here he uses a crude vernacular term such as many nations use when referring to those they regard as inferior neighbors.

89

But the woman takes Jesus on and says that even the dogs (Gentiles) eat the scraps that fall from the children (of Israel)'s table. And in this, which some would see as a churlish riposte, he sees a statement of faith to which he can only respond by healing her child.

Thirdly we have the story of a healing that is requested by a man who is not a Jew. The story of the centurion is found in Matthew *(8:5–13)* and Luke *(7:1–10)* and each account has some original features.

The common ground is that the centurion comes to ask Jesus to heal his servant. Recently some scholars have indicated that the word used could refer equally to a domestic aide or to a younger man who was the centurion's partner. If, indeed, the latter were the case, that might help explain his reticence to have Jesus visit the household in case it in any way compromised Jesus. But irrespective of the status of the sufferer, Jesus is taken aback at the faith of the man who, using a military analogy, believes that as he commands men, so Jesus can command illness.

Jesus, astonished at his declaration of belief, says, "Truly I tell you, I have never found such faith in all of Israel." This expression is sufficient to indicate that the centurion was not a Jew and in all probability would be a Roman. Luke endorses this with the information that the Jewish elders made an urgent appeal to Jesus to respond positively to the man's request, " ... for he is a friend of our nation and it is he who built our synagogue." Matthew, in his account, records words of Jesus that slightly foreshadow the parable of the Sheep and the Goats, in which nations are judged not according to their religious affiliation but according to how they practice social justice and show generosity to the disadvantaged.

Many . . . will come from the east and west to sit with
Abraham, and Isaac, and Jacob at the banquet in the
kingdom of Heaven. But those who were born to the
kingdom will be thrown out into the dark.

(Matthew 8:11–12)

Here again is evidence of Jesus' conviction, which is an offense
to his listeners, that their espoused religion and treasured
nation are no guarantee of salvation.

The icon of hospitality

Finally we should remember that fictional character whom
Jesus chose to represent the model of care and hospitality.

In all Jesus' parables there is an element of surprise and
occasionally offense. Many of the stories have an illogicality
within them. For example, few fathers whose sons have
squandered half their savings welcome such aberrant
offspring back with a party. Again, irrespective of the century,
it does not bode well for industrial relations if a man hiring
laborers pays the same wage to those who have worked for a
few hours as to those who have been on the job all day.

To the first hearers of the parable of the Good Samaritan
(Luke 10:30–37), the title itself would seem something of an
oxymoron. Just as there are Jewish lepers who don't return
to thank God when they have been cured, so there are Jewish
religious dignitaries who would rather avoid the victim of a
mugging than help the injured person. And just as a Samaritan
leper expresses exceptional gratitude, so it is a Samaritan
traveller who cares for the injured man, transports him on
his own donkey, and pays for his board and lodging with his
own money.

This is the hero whose ethnicity alone suggested to the Jews that he was not one they would want to emulate. Malina and Rohrbaugh (see pp. 45–46) suggest three reasons as to why the hero in the parable would be less than attractive:

a. the Samaritan was probably a trader, therefore of a dishonorable fraternity;
b. the victim was ritually unclean, contaminating whomever touched him;
c. inns were establishments notorious for being run by and hosting people of bad reputation.

But there is perhaps also a sting in the tail of this parable.

The prelude to it was a lawyer asking Jesus, "Who is my neighbor?" After telling the parable, Jesus asks the lawyer who was neighbor to the man who was mugged. The lawyer replies, "The one who showed him kindness." Jesus then enjoins him to "go and do as he did." But does that imply simply that the lawyer should help people in distress? Or—much more controversial—does it mean that in addition to being extravagantly kind, he also has to love Samaritans and whomever else helps the distressed. For indeed, the initial question was "Who is the neighbor I have to love?" And the answer is not "Go and do likewise." The answer, on the basis of the parable, has to be, "The person, irrespective of their race, who does good to others."

In societies that are increasingly multicultural, where practitioners of world religions—Islam, Judaism, Buddhism, Christianity, Hinduism—can be found in all major world cities, one of the great strengths of the Christian faith is that its founder recognized that faith was not the property of one sect, but was a potential in all people. When a Muslim's faith leads him or her to so something sacrificial, it is not an inferior act because it is done by a non-Christian. It is something for which Christians should be grateful. For Jesus did not come to say that either the ancient Hebrews or the fledgling Christians were morally and spiritually superior because they were devoted to the true God. He came to recognize and to indicate that God was the ground of all goodness, the quality of which manifests in people of all religions and of none.

This does not undermine Christ's claim of uniqueness. Rather it endorses it, for he is uniquely able to recognize and to love the good in those who are "not belonging to this fold" *(John 10:16)*.

Chapter eight

Business lunches

The thin man

Why do we always make Jesus out to be undernourished? Is it because he was the son of a woman who is depicted as keeping her teenage figure well into her old age? Did he secretly emulate the diet of his cousin, John the Baptist, who survived on locusts and wild honey? Or is it nothing to do with his genes? Maybe he made himself anorexic. Or perhaps because he had only one garment, he never risked getting too big for it.

We shall explore more plausible reasons later. But let's begin by looking at the evidence.

For many people, the only meals they remember Jesus participating in are the feeding of a crowd of five thousand and a meal in an upstairs room commonly referred to as the Last Supper. Even academics who study the scriptures seem to be oblivious when it comes to Jesus' gastronomic enthusiasm.

Hence James P. Mackey in *Jesus, the Man and the Myth: A Contemporary Christology* comments:

> Apart from the Last Supper, there is not much detail in the New Testament on Jesus' practice of table fellowship.
>
> (Mackey, *Jesus, the Man*, 147)

Below is a list of occasions when Jesus was present while food was eaten. We cannot say for sure that he physically

95

partook in every instance. But from what we know about Jewish hospitality, it is highly unlikely that any guest would be present in a host's house for any length of time and not be offered a meal. Those occasions that are slightly dubious are asterisked (*), but, as can be seen, they are in the minority.

- Passover in Jerusalem—when he ran away from his parents/*Luke 2:41–52*
- Sustenance in the desert provided by angels/*Matthew 4:11*
- Wedding feast at Cana/*John 2:1–10*
- Peter's house, where he is waited on by the recovered mother-in-law/*Mark 1:29–31*
- Meal in the house of the tax collector called both Matthew and Levi/*Matthew 9:9–13*
- *Cornfields where his disciples help themselves/*Mark 2:23–26*
- Village of Sychar to which his disciples brought food/ *John 4:31*
- *Jairus' house where he tells the parents to give their daughter something to eat/*Mark 5:35–43*
- Feeding of the five thousand/*John 6:1–13*
- Meal in the house of Simon the Pharisee/*Luke 7:36–50*
- Unknown location where the disciples eat food with unwashed hands/*Mark 7:1–8*
- *House in Tyre where possibly a meal-table is set/ *Mark 7:24–30*
- Feeding of the four thousand/*Mark 8:1–10*
- *Home of Martha and Mary/*Luke 10:38–42*
- House of a Pharisee where Jesus does not wash his hands/*Luke 11:37–40*
- Sabbath meal in the house of a leading Pharisee/*Luke 14:1–24*

- House of Zacchaeus into which Jesus invites himself/ *Luke 19:1–10*
- Meal in the home of Lazarus, Martha and Mary/*John 12:1–11*
- House of Simon the Leper/*Matthew 26:6–13*
- The Last Supper/*Mark 14:17–25*
- Meal after the journey to Emmaus/*Luke 24:28–32*
- Food eaten by Jesus in the upstairs room/*Luke 24:36–43*
- Breakfast barbecue on the beach/*John 21:9–14*

Here are up to twenty-three occasions when Jesus and food are at close quarters. We could stop here and ponder whether there is any other figure in world history who is so frequently referred to as being in the proximity of a meal table. The issue becomes more significant when we remember that the Gospels do not provide us with a biography of Jesus, but with a collection of reminiscences of what he did, said and meant to people, put together in four books, three of which are closely connected, and the shortest of which can be read in an hour.

If this is the evidence, why do we imagine Jesus to be more abstemious than gregarious, showing more evidence of the need for food than the satisfaction of being well fed?

Reasons for slenderness

There are a number of commonly suggested reasons with which I shall try to deal respectfully.

1. He walked a lot.

We have absolutely no evidence for believing that Jesus travelled more than anyone else. He did not go on sponsored walks for charity, ending up with blisters on his feet. He went from village to village, and—as when he met the Samaritan woman at the well—sometimes enjoyed people's company so much that he changed his schedule and stayed an extra day or two *(John 4:40)*.

2. People were undernourished in those days.

The archaeological evidence is to the contrary. People had a reasonable diet of fruit, vegetables, seeds, fish and olive oil. The World Health Organisation recommends that a healthy diet consist of 1500 to 1900 calories per day. It is reckoned that Jesus and his companions would have had a daily intake of around 1800 calories.

In addition, although he shows evidence of tiredness, neither he nor the disciples ever say that they are hungry.

3. Jesus would have had to lead an ascetic life because he was a holy man.

Jesus never alluded to such a compulsion. In fact that was why people distrusted him. They had seen the asceticism of John, which led them to presume that he was off his head. In contrast the gregariousness of Jesus led to rumors about his being "a glutton and a drinker" *(Matthew 11:2–19)*.

4. He was known as "a man of sorrows and acquainted with grief, an object from which people turn away their eyes."

No, he was not. That allusion does not come from the Gospel but from the prophecy of Isaiah, chapter 53. It depicts God's servant, sometimes taken to be the nation Israel, and sometimes associated with a single messianic figure. While it particularly foreshadows Jesus' passion and death, it cannot be taken as a commentary on his whole life. And it is a defamation of Jesus' character to represent him as someone who was constantly worried and burdened by the woes of life, when he consistently encouraged others to trust God and get on with living.

5. He is always pictured that way.

This is absolutely true, but that does not make it right. As we noted earlier, artists and poets have been amazingly restrictive in the way they depict Jesus. Somehow it has been more important to associate him with the tragedy of life than with its enjoyment, even though he specifically said that it was for the latter that he came. Did he not say, "I have spoken thus to you, so that my joy may be in you, and your joy complete" *(John 15:11)*? Or is that a misreading of the Gospel?

6. We need a skinny Savior.

Few will admit to this, but there may be a curious psychological aversion to the notion that the Savior of the world liked food and enjoyed company. Sometimes we imagine that the most heroic figures are those who display a solidarity with the oppressed through adopting a frugal lifestyle. That may be a reflection of Gandhi, but it is not so evident in Tutu and Mandela. In any case, is it helpful to the poor to be championed by someone who role-plays their poverty, or to be represented by someone whose solidarity is not in doubt and who safeguards his or her health?

Or is it that the hidden ascetic in us has worked out that it is cheaper to fast than to feast?

Before moving to discuss why Jesus is so frequently found at meal tables, we should take a quick and less detailed look at what he says about food, for allusions to eating and nourishment seem to pepper and salt so much of his conversation.

Here, for example, is a list of parables in which food plays an important part:

• The Sower	*Mark 4:3*
• The Sprouting Seed	*Mark 4:26*
• The Mustard Seed	*Mark 4:31*
• The Yeast in the Dough	*Matthew 13:33*
• The Fish in the Net	*Matthew 13:47*
• The Good Samaritan	*Luke 10:34*
• The Neighbor Borrowing Food	*Luke 11:05*
• The Rich Man's Barns	*Luke 12:16*
• The Watchful Servants	*Luke 12:37*
• The Fig Tree	*Luke 13:6*
• Seating Arrangements	*Luke 14:7*
• The Great Feast	*Luke 14:16*
• The Prodigal Son	*Luke 15:11*
• The Rich Man and Lazarus	*Luke 16:19*
• The Vineyard	*Mark 12:1*
• The Wedding Banquet	*Matthew 22:2*
• The Wise Virgins	*Matthew 25:1*
• The Sheep and the Goats	*Matthew 25:31*

Sixteen parables, and that list does not exhaust the pithy and profound statements that most of us could remember given little prompting. Here are some, just from Luke's Gospel:

• New skins for new wine	*5:38*
• Each tree is known by its fruit	*6:44*
• The crop is heavy but laborers are few	*10:2*
• Give us each day our daily bread	*11:3*
• Would a father give his son a snake for a fish?	*11:11*
• Don't worry about what to eat and drink	*12:29*

- Don't just invite your friends to dinner   *14:12*
- What use is salt if it loses its flavor?   *14:34*
- A servant after work still has to make the meal *17:8*
- Where the carcass is, the vultures will gather   *17:37*
- There will be famines   *21:11*

We could add to these the sayings of Jesus and the ensuing controversies when he speaks of himself as the true bread and the true vine. There is no paucity of evidence. The wonder is that we seem so reticent to admit to Jesus' fascination with and passion for food.

Reasons for eating

So why is there so much mention of food and so many meals? Here we have to mix a little theology and a little conjecture, but all based on biblical evidence.

1. Meals are great levellers.

At a table, everyone is important. All share the same food and—unless it is a very formal affair—anyone can speak. There is something about the physical proximity of people and the activity of eating and drinking that enables communication and develops community.

What would enable Jesus to get close to the marginalized? Standing in a pulpit above and beyond their reach? Or sitting in a tax collector's house among his colleagues and some hookers who were considered the trash of society?

What would enable Jesus to discover the real men behind the role-playing legalists? Asking the Pharisees to debate with him in open court? Or accepting an invitation to dine?

What would let Jesus affirm that the resurrected Lazarus was back to normal? Asking after him through a third party? Or having a meal in his home as he had often done before?

What would let Jesus prove to his disciples that it was the same person who had risen as had been crucified? An exegesis of prophecies that pointed in that direction? Or seeing him eat food in the way he had so often done before?

We all know the way in which a shared meal can break down barriers. Indeed I would argue that the success of the Alpha Course and other such educational endeavors is as much to do with strangers sitting down and eating together as it is with faith being discussed openly.

I know as much from my own experience. Years ago I was asked to chair the music committee of my denomination. It had hitherto met in a broom cupboard at a time when most members could not attend. It therefore did nothing. I suggested that if I were to convene the committee, we should meet at a time suitable to all (which meant evenings), and in a central venue where we could eat first. So for several years we met at Scottish Churches' House in Dunblane. From six o'clock to seven we ate, and from seven till nine o'clock or later we did business. There was never any contentiousness, rarely if ever the need for a vote, and seldom a meeting when more than two members were absent. And in those years, not only did the group begin to resurrect interest in the music of the church, but they genuinely enjoyed working together. The good humor and the kindly friendship initiated there still remains over a decade later.

2. Meals are where children and adults sit together.

This may seem a minor issue, but in the present climate it is a major concern.

On several occasions Jesus talks about children and food, and we discover that children were present at the feeding of the five thousand. In the house in Tyre where he converses with the Syro-Phoenician woman, there is an allusion to the children's food that drops from the table and is eaten by the dogs. And certainly at every Passover children would not only be present, but would participate in the ritual surrounding the food. We need to recapture that sense of all ages being present at the table today.

Several years ago, a school group came to the MacLeod Centre on Iona. After their first evening, two questions were being asked by the young teenagers: "Are we always going to have home-cooked meals?" and "Are we always going to sit at a table?"

When I asked their teacher why the second question was asked, she said that probably over a third of these kids had no table in their home. They would either eat a meal on their lap in front of the television, or take it upstairs and eat it in front of their computer. The potential of the meal table as the place to exchange news, express disquiet, learn how to manage anger, and meet guests—all of this was absent in the lives of these teenagers.

Coincidentally, around the time of this incident, I read two articles in American newspapers. One indicated that research showed that unsociable behavior in people in their late teens and early twenties was directly related to the lack of a meal table in their childhood homes. This was as true for the affluent as for the poor. The other report indicated that in furnishing the majority of American households, the first object to be purchased is the television, and the last the kitchen table.

3. Meals are times of giving and receiving.

We need not dwell too much on this, except to say that there is a mutuality about dining together. For the host, a meal means expending money, time, energy and imagination to provide a meal for guests. But when it comes to eating, there is an expectation that the guests will supply conversation. And in that mutual exchange there is the possibility for learning to happen, understanding to grow and appreciation to be shown.

It may well have been at meals that Jesus heard snippets of conversation or testimonies of life experience, which would either provide illustrations for teaching or suggest issues that he needed to address at a later date. It is quite conceivable that at a meal table an older woman might have said to Jesus, "Do you know what happened last week? I lost a coin from my bracelet." And then, as she tells the story, he finds in it a parable of God's kingdom.

Is it equally conceivable that at another meal, a younger woman says to him, "There's no way I would go to bed with a man who I'm not married to but I can't do a thing about these men on the building site who keep leering and whistling at me." And so he quickens his thinking about how to secure male respect for attractive women.

And, in all this, he allows people to give to him their experiences, their secrets, their stories; for he has come to let people know that God relies on them.

4. Hospitality is a cardinal virtue ...

... not an optional extra. Jesus would know this from the womb. Food and feeding were and still are important facets of Jewish culture. The Hebrew scriptures are replete with stories of hospitality—from Abraham entertaining angels in his garden, through David allowing his troops to eat the sacred bread when hungry, to the book of Ecclesiastes, which extols the delights of food and drink.

But more than that, hospitality is at the heart of God. Indeed, though it is often unrecognized, the world's favorite psalm has God depicted as a host. Psalm 23 has two images of the Lord. The more popular is that of the Shepherd, but in verse five another image replaces the first:

> You spread a table for me ...
> You anoint my head with oil ...
> My cup overflows ...

This is a God who models hospitality in order that those made in God's image might do likewise. And the kindness God models should not, in ecclesiastical settings, be limited to what is called "eucharistic hospitality," i.e., whether or not we can share communion together. It has to do with how we welcome people, how we affirm people, how we enable sociability and sharing, and also whether what we eat is wholesome.

5. Food is a justice issue.

It might seem appropriate to ally this statement to the feeding of the five thousand. But I refrain from that because I am not sure that this is primarily what the miracle demonstrates.

Rather, we should be aware that when Jesus says that he has come to fulfil the law and the prophets, there is within that an implicit expectation that the social welfare provided for the impoverished as required by the Law, and the indictments against social injustice articulated by the Prophets are not surpassed by Jesus but are part and parcel of the gospel. Two out of many illustrations will suffice.

Leviticus 19 is a portion of the Law that, along with outlawing theft, deception and other perversions of justice, also forbids the harvesting of crops right to the edge of the field. This margin has to be left for the poor to glean, a requirement that was of particular benefit to the widowed Ruth *(Ruth 2:1–3)*.

Amos is particularly virulent in his denunciation of the wealthy whose pampered existences depend on their denying the right of the impoverished and, indeed, passing legislation that increases their likelihood of going hungry:

> You that turn justice to poison
> and thrust righteousness to the ground ...
> [who] levy taxes on the poor
> and extort a tribute of grain from them. *(Amos 5:7, 11)*

Other instances of the same kind of writing are innumerable and Jesus stands foursquare in this tradition. We know this from some of his stories. The rich man who fills his barns with corn, irrespective of the needs of anyone else, is doomed by his maker *(Luke 12:13–21)*. The rich man who sees the beggar at his gate and never moves to alleviate his plight is severely penalized in the afterlife *(Luke 16:19–31)*. And, on a more corporate level, nations that fail to feed the hungry are damned on the day of judgment *(Matthew 25:31–46)*.

When read aloud in conjunction with current debates on the global food situation, it is clear that the injustice against which the law, the prophets and Jesus protested is still alive and kicking. It is present in the unfair way in which wealthy nations subsidize particular crops (such as sugar cane) and sell them in the open market in competition with similar crops from poorer nations that cannot offer their farmers subsidies.

It is present in the way Western traders sell chemical fertilizer and genetically modified seeds to farmers in Africa and Asia, irrespective of the long-term damage such commodities may cause the soil and the local economy, let alone people's health. It is present in the way in which basic commodities have prices that inflate and deflate at a whim, according to the stock and futures markets, over which developing nations have no control. (A pertinent example is Thai rice, which in the first three months of 2008 increased by $360/ton, only to drop from that giddy height a few months later.)

It is present in the mad rush to take over food-producing land in poor countries so that wealthier nations may grow crops that can be turned into bio-fuel to supplement falling and prohibitively priced oil supplies.

It is present in the contrast between one in three children in the USA being obese and one in three children in many African nations being on the verge of starvation. It is present in the contrast between the rich world, where 10–20% of a household income is spent on food, and the poor world, where it is up to 70%. Food is a justice issue.

6. Food is meant for all to enjoy.

It was a crowd of teenagers who unearthed this insight, the same group mentioned in Chapter Two who articulated questions they wanted to ask Jesus. One of the questions was: How did it feel when you sent out five loaves and two fishes and received back twelve baskets of leftovers?

I decided to explore the story of the feeding of the five thousand by way of a meditation in which I would retell the story and ask questions at pertinent moments, allowing the participants to fill in the blanks so to speak.

I began by asking them to shut their eyes and imagine they were in a village in Palestine where the news went round that a famous orator was coming to speak in a field outside the town. Having decided to go and hear him, what preparations had to be made? Did people go alone or in groups? Were children taken or child-care arranged? How long did they think they would be away for and did that make any difference?

On and on the meditation went in the same way. A little bit of the story and then questions that needed a personal, silent response.

When it came to the actual miracle, I asked how they felt seeing a young boy offering Jesus his lunch. Did they feel sentimental, or admiring, or embarrassed, or challenged?

When it came to the food being distributed, I asked them what happened when somebody passed one of the baskets to them over their shoulder. When it was all over and they were walking back home, I asked them how their opinion of Jesus had been shaped by what they experienced.

Then, when the meditation came to its end, I began to ask again the questions people had pondered individually and this time they responded aloud. There was no collaboration and, as

I had never done this before, I had no idea of the outcome.

When we got to the bit about the baskets being passed, and what did they do when one arrived in their group, the vast majority said, "I put something into it." "Where did you get food from?" I asked, and a girl replied, "I went with my four children, and because I had no idea how long we would be away, I took stuff for them to eat."

"Where did you keep it?" I asked, and she replied, "That's for me to know and you to imagine!"

Most of the others made a similar response. When they saw the young boy naively giving all he had to Jesus, and Jesus accepting the gift and blessing it with complete seriousness, and then sharing it with everyone, even the hard-hearted were moved to be generous and demonstrate by a new open-handedness that food was for sharing.

I had never thought of this before. It was that crowd of teenagers who opened up this profound insight that the feeding of the five thousand has more to do with Jesus miraculously changing human selfishness into generosity than it has to do with any magical change in the physical properties of a young boy's lunch.

Were the church, for whatever reason, banned from displaying publicly the sign of the cross, the table would be the most immediate domestic symbol to associate with Jesus. Not the eucharistic table, but the regular meal table. This is not to detract from the importance of Holy Communion. Rather it is to see it in a larger context ... that of one of a succession of meals in which Jesus fondly engaged with those whom he loved and those with whom he longed to connect. When we review the other meals Jesus is recorded as sharing, we will find aspects of them that resonate in the Eucharist and give it a deeper meaning than that of a memorial feast.

So, when next we think of Jesus, let us forgo the jaded, unbiblical images of the hungry man with the sad face, and rather think of Christ as the gregarious guest, the contented diner, the generous host, the breakfast cook.

Chapter nine

Righteous indignation

Embattled in the bush

This was too much to believe. Indeed it was offensive to the man, and he told me so.

It was in a bush town in Australia, of perhaps five thousand inhabitants, and I had agreed to participate in an evening event for the Uniting Church congregation. Over dinner, the minister asked whether I would ever consider leading a men's Bible study. I responded positively, since it was not a request I often received. Then he asked if I would be prepared to do that very thing at six o'clock the next morning.

Having shown enthusiasm, it was hard to back-pedal and be reticent. So I agreed, although there was little time to work up anything new. I decided, therefore, to share with the men the passage of John's Gospel that I was reading for my own purposes at the time. It was chapter 11 where the first 43 verses tell the story of the raising of Lazarus.

I love John's Gospel and I love this miracle story. It is so detailed. It's like a film script. The action happens in four different locations. It tells of Martha, who in Luke's Gospel is depicted as the less devout of two sisters, showing more faith in Jesus than her sister Mary. It has lots of contrasts: puzzlement and certainty, silence and noise, what seems like inertia and movement. And it depicts Jesus as someone who was not exempt from feeling deep human emotions.

The next morning at six o'clock there were around fourteen men in a comfortable room in the church. Coffee was available as we gathered. There were a couple of tradesmen, one or two teachers, a consultant in dental medicine, an unemployed man, an accountant and others whose employments I can't remember.

I indicated that to begin with I'd read the passage for consideration. That might help the Aussies to become accustomed to my accent. I suggested that if anything I read was unclear, or if a word or phrase stuck in their mind, we'd deal with that first. So I read, slowly and clearly, and then asked if anything needed to be clarified.

The consultant spoke up. "Could you read again the verse that dealt with Jesus' reaction to the people who were with Mary?" he asked. "Certainly," I said and read the verse from *The Revised English Bible* translation:

> When Jesus saw [Mary] weeping and the Jews who had come with her weeping, he was moved with indignation and deeply distressed. *(John 11:33)*

"What does that mean—indignation?" asked the consultant. "It means he was angry, very angry," I replied. "How come?" said the consultant. "Because it was an untimely death," I suggested. "Jesus loved Lazarus. He was probably one of his close friends. And suddenly and unexpectedly he dies. It might have been an aneurism. We don't know. And Mary—the one who had all the faith—she's in a state. And so are her friends. And possibly Jesus feels that the pressure is on for him to fix it. He's livid."

"That can't possibly be true," said the consultant. "Why not?" I asked. "My friend," he said slightly patronizingly, "I have been a Christian for over forty years and I have never known Jesus Christ to be angry." And then he asked, "What does it say in the Greek?"

"My man," I replied, "you're lucky that I can read the English never mind the Greek at this time in the morning. But if we did have the Greek available, we'd find that it is a very rarely used word."

And so it is. The Greek is *enebrimaisato* ... a word used only in this verse and there is no unanimity in translations. The *NRSV* suggests "greatly disturbed in spirit"; the *New American Bible* suggests "perturbed."

Perhaps I went a bit too far in saying that Jesus was "livid," but what is certainly implicit in the text is a mixture of confusion, upset, anger and uneasiness.

Shaped by song

I did not get into a contentious argument with the consultant (it was too early in the morning!). But I did speak to him later, for he was an earnest believer and was clearly upset at the notion that Jesus could have lost his composure or expressed even mild anger. The reason for this went back to hymns that this man had sung in his childhood and not just of the "gentle Jesus, meek and mild" variety, although he had sung plenty of these.

The hymnal he had grown up with was called *The Revised Church Hymnary*, published in Britain in 1927 and explicitly for use in Presbyterian churches in Scotland, England, Ireland, Wales, Australia, New Zealand and South Africa. As was common until relatively recently, the hymns of Jesus' life were

113

few in number in comparison to those dealing with his birth and death. Among the scanty texts to do with Jesus' ministry was one the consultant remembered and liked. It began:

> What grace, O Lord, and beauty shone
> around thy steps below.

Then comes the fatal verse:

> For ever on thy burdened heart
> a weight of sorrow hung,
> yet no ungentle, murmuring word
> escaped thy silent tongue.

On that aberrant text hung the man's belief that Jesus could never have been angry. Just as bad, however is the ensuing verse:

> Thy foes might hate, despise, revile,
> thy friends unfaithful prove;
> unwearied in forgiveness still,
> thy heart could only love.

One wonders whether the author of such lines heard nothing but soothing tones in Jesus' voice when he told the Devil and Peter to get behind him, and when he accused the Pharisees of being snakes. Yet even in the devotional ditties of the twenty-first century, Jesus—whether depicted in heaven or on earth—seems to have his strong emotions constantly subdued or on holiday. He never gets excited, raises his voice, expresses displeasure. His demeanor is the emotional equivalent of the color grey.

Jesus and just(ifiable) anger

To some extent, this passive depiction of Jesus is understandable even if not desirable. For some it is a welcome contrast to the impressions of God in the Hebrew scriptures as one who expresses no small amount of displeasure, calling privileged and uncaring women "cows" and offering to ransack the peace and quiet of the privileged who fleece the poor. It is as if Jesus and God play good cop/bad cop. That may be a presumption that armchair theologians and wordsmiths have about the relationship between the Father and the Son. But it cannot be sustained from Jesus' own words. For as John's Gospel indicates on several occasions, Jesus' testimony is "The Father and I are one" *(John 10:30).*

But can we have an angry Jesus? Would that not put people off religion? I think it's a risk not only worth taking, but one that is necessary.

We have to do this because Jesus frequently exhibits anger, although for many believers the sole occasion on which that was shown was the incident referred to as "The Cleansing of the Temple."

All four Gospels mention it. John locates it towards the beginning of Jesus' ministry, the others a few days before his arrest. He is recorded as displaying anger in both word and action. He accuses the temple authorities in these terms:

> Scripture says, "My house shall be called a house of prayer"; but you are making it a bandits' cave.
>
> *(Matthew 21:13)*

Matthew records that Jesus "drove out all who were buying and selling in the temple precincts; he upset the tables of the money-changers and the seats of the dealers in pigeons" *(Matthew 21:12).* John is even more graphic:

> He made a whip of cords and drove them out of the
> temple, sheep, cattle, and all. He upset the tables of the
> money-changers, scattering their coins. Then he turned
> on the dealers in pigeons. *(John 2:15–16a)*

Are these the typical actions of a mild-mannered aesthete? Indeed, are these the actions of someone exhibiting anger for the first time in his life? I suggest not. There is precision in what happens, as well as the quoting of scriptural warrant.

Even with our fondest desire to see Jesus as a mild-mannered individual, we cannot imagine him speaking his words of censure in gentle tones, or disrupting temple trade and furnishings with the minimum of gesticulation.

And the reason for what seems like irregular behavior was not personal pique or some recent criticism that irked him into retaliation. Rather, he is incensed by the injustice of an economic system, condoned by the temple authorities, that discriminates against the poor—both in the extortionate rate of exchange levied by money-changers, and the arbitrary cost of animals for sacrificial purposes.

To do nothing, to remain calm in the face of this iniquity, would be to condone the discriminatory practices.

Other displays of anger

However, it would be wrong to imagine that this was the only occasion on which Jesus expressed what we might call "righteous indignation."

In Luke's Gospel there is the account of the healing of a woman who had been crippled for eighteen years *(Luke 13:10–17)*. We have already considered this incident in a previous chapter. But what we may here note is how Jesus responds to his critic, the president of the synagogue, who was "indignant" with Jesus for healing on the Sabbath. The man intervenes and says to the congregation, "There are six working days: come and be cured on one of them, and not on the sabbath."

These words are not addressed to Jesus, but he takes it upon himself to reply, for here he identifies a lingering hypocrisy that many of the so-called guardians of faith exhibit.

> "What hypocrites you are!" he said. "Is there a single one of you who does not loose his ox or his donkey from its stall and take it out to water on the sabbath? And here is this woman, a daughter of Abraham, who has been bound by Satan for eighteen long years: was it not right for her to be loosed from her bonds on the sabbath?"
>
> *(Luke 13:15–16)*

Put in these graphic terms, there is something clearly monstrous about denying a human being made in the image of God the liberation given to a domestic animal. Here, again, we have Jesus expressing outrage, because to refrain from doing so would be to take a position of complicity.

In another account of a healing in a synagogue where his critics are keen to censure what is happening, Mark records that Jesus looked "round at them with anger and sorrow at their obstinate stupidity" *(Mark 3:5)*.

And, in this context, we might remember the catalogue of hypocrisy with which he confronts the Pharisees in

117

Matthew's Gospel:

> Alas for you, scribes and Pharisees, hypocrites! You shut the door of the kingdom of Heaven in people's faces; you do not enter yourselves but you prevent others from doing so. You travel over land and sea to make one convert; then you make him twice as fit for hell as you are. You clean the outside of the dish, but leave the inside full of greed and self-indulgence.
>
> *(Matthew 23:13, 15, 25, alt.)*

Luke, who records similar words, has a lawyer intervening to intercede for the Pharisees who are suffering a verbal onslaught, only to find that Jesus' anger deftly transfers to the objector's own profession:

> Alas for you lawyers also! You load men with intolerable burdens, and will not lift a finger to lighten the load. *(Luke 11:46)*

These passages simply cannot be read *sotto voce*. Jesus is not an exemplar of mealy-mouthed pleasantries at such moments, but a scathing advocate for the marginalized and persecuted, exposing the unquestioned cant and privilege of their oppressors. One can almost hear the synagogue congregation cheering Jesus to the rafters, and the witnesses to his verbal flaying of the Pharisees and lawyers unable to suppress their delight.

For Jesus, neutrality was not an option when confronted with shameless injustice. If a situation required him to raise his voice or use colorful vocabulary to unstitch the smugness of his critics, he did not hold back.

Personal animosity

On a more personal level, Jesus expresses anger at individuals who should know better than to do or say the things that he observes. Both the Devil and Peter hear the rebuke, "Out of my sight, Satan!" *(Matthew 4:10; 16:23)*.

Then there are at least four occasions when it is the full complement of the apostles who are the objects of his anger. The first time is when they are all in a boat caught in a storm. The disciples panic and waken the sleeping Jesus. He deals with the storm. But he also deals with them, just as severely: "Why are you such cowards? . . . How little faith you have!" *(Matthew 8:23–27)*.

A while later, in the same Gospel, a man brings to Jesus his sick son whom the disciples have been unable to cure. His words to them are not exactly warm and welcoming, "What an unbelieving and perverse generation! How long shall I be with you? How long must I endure you?" *(Matthew 17:17)*.

We also have the incident where—perhaps out of a desire to protect Jesus from too much public exposure or engagement in matters of little importance—the disciples rebuke people who want to bring children to Jesus. His response to them: When Jesus saw it he was indignant *(Mark 10:13–16)*.

Finally, there is the unusual incident in which the disciples discover that the inhabitants of a Samaritan village to which Jesus is heading are unwilling to offer him hospitality. In a moment of bravado, they offer "to call down fire from heaven to consume them" *(Luke 9:54)*. What does Jesus do, whose affection for non-Jews we have already witnessed? "He turned and rebuked [the disciples]" *(Luke 9:55)*.

These incidents are not so much concerned with social injustice, although elements of this can be discerned in each. More clearly, Jesus is venting exasperation at people whom he believes should know better. And perhaps the measure of his affection for his disciples was that he did not spare them his frustration just as he did not spare them his encouragement, support and love.

Why do we deny anger in Jesus?

However, to admit that these and other instances are clear indications of anger within Jesus, while a liberation to some, is disturbing to others. This is not the Jesus of whom we sang in childhood. No. But this is the Jesus to whom the Gospels witness.

The root of our unease, if we feel it, may be twofold. We may be dealing with the shattering of a long-held conviction that Jesus was always pleasant and was firmly against exhibitions of anger. Indeed, we might even quote Jesus' words: Anyone who nurses anger against his brother must be brought to justice *(Matthew 5:22)*.

But this quotation is not about the anger, which is a response to injustice or stupidity. This anger, which Jesus proscribes, is of the nature of brooding resentment that sours human relationships the longer it is coveted. Robert Burns, in his poem *Tam O' Shanter*, has a lovely phrase describing the wife of the hapless Tam. She "nurses her wrath to keep it warm."

A second reason for reticence to see anger in Jesus could be that we may have known it in ourselves as something that is ugly whether expressed against us or expressed by us. Some people, including myself, are not very good at expressing anger. For me, it is because I grew up in a household where my parents never expressed anger to each other in front of their children.

So while, as a child, I was occasionally the object of their displeasure, I never saw a model of how to express anger responsibly to another adult. My first attempts at it were woeful. I felt tongue-tied and guilty. But later, when gross injustice was being shown to someone for whom I had responsibility, I raised my voice and, despite perspiring profusely, managed forcibly and successfully to argue my case.

I think that for Jesus—as for the writers of the psalms of complaint—there was a necessity to articulate what was genuinely and justly felt. Otherwise, to nurse it would be both to magnify its importance out of proportion and also to defer the possibility of articulating the anger responsibly.

Jesus' anger is always rooted in love and justice. He did not continually disparage his disciples. He reproved them because they needed it, and then they all got on with the job at hand. Nor did he hate the Pharisees and lawyers. He accepted hospitality from some, and could identify their sincerity when it was evident.

Anger is not the opposite of love, just as doubt is not the opposite of faith. Indifference in both instances is the real enemy.

Chapter ten

Giggling for God

Evidence of divine humor

The suggested proof that God has a sense of humor is often self-referential. People recount some odd or ridiculous situation in which they once found themselves and see that as evidence that the hand of heaven was behind the farce. More worryingly, some priests and ministers see their vocation and ordination as proof of levity on the part of their Maker.

I want to suggest that evidence of God's humor is a bit more objective. In fact, it is one of the first characteristics of God recorded in the Bible. We discover it in that odd story of Abraham and Sarah, the couple who in their retirement years were gradually made aware that God had chosen them to begin a new nation.

It began when, aged 99, Abraham laughed at God's suggestion that he and his hitherto barren wife were going to become parents. No reprimand was given for this doubting of divine purpose. Perhaps God did not hear the laughter because, "Abraham bowed low" *(Genesis 17:17a)*.

Sarah, aged 89, did not get off so easily. She giggled as she eavesdropped from behind a tent flap. Her husband was entertaining angels in the garden and she was cooking a meal. She overheard one of the celestial beings say that in a year he'd pay a return visit, by which time the elderly couple would have had a son. In an act of what seems like chauvinism, God, who had no complaint when Abraham laughed, took him to task for his wife's stifled guffaw. She,

123

of course, denied that any such noise had been made by her, but in nine months' time the smile was on the other side of her face, and she gave birth to a boy *(Genesis 18:1–15; 21:1–8).*

"God has made laughter for me," was Sarah's response to the birth of Isaac, and in that there is a play on words, for Isaac—the name given to the child—is the Hebrew word for laughter. And it was a woman who saw laughter-making as an attribute of God.

But what about Jesus, the human face of God on earth?

Did Jesus laugh?

Just as there is a reticence to countenance Jesus as a *bon viveur*, there is a similar hesitation in seeing him as one who—despite being of the lineage of Abraham and Sarah—enjoyed good humor.

Empirical evidence of that can be seen in something that happened almost a decade ago. An Australian entrepreneur and devout Christian had the idea of mounting an exhibition called "Jesus Laughed" at the Fringe of the Edinburgh International Festival. He asked a younger colleague to search for artists in the English-speaking world who had painted or who would paint Jesus laughing. The response was negligible. There was little evidence among religious artists that such a depiction had been attempted and nobody seemed attracted to the idea. The exhibition eventually opened under the title "Jesus—Laughing and Loving." The latter activity dominated the show.

Now, there are some reasons for this that are extraneous to our present pursuit, but worth mentioning in passing. There are actually very few portraits of anyone laughing, because as distinct from frowning, laughing is not something a model can sustain for an hour. Laughter is very elusive. It is like a wave that crests and falls very quickly. We know this when we look at group photographs in which everyone is in stitches apart from one figure who seems to be in pain. The likelihood is that her or his laugh has crested before that of the others and the facial muscles, now relaxing, are not at their most photogenic.

That having been said, can we with any confidence state that there is any evidence in the Gospels that Jesus had a sense of humor? I believe we can make such a claim and point to evidence, but first one other necessary diversion regarding the nature of humor.

A humorous diversion

Humor is amazingly culturally bound. It is an in-group thing that cannot always be communicated from one society to another, let alone from one language to another. Many of us have realized the latter reality when telling a joke in English to someone who has a different mother-tongue. They don't get it. So we tell it again, a little louder and with our shoulders shaking at the punchline. They—who may be German, Japanese or Peruvian—smile and make some sound suggestive of pleasure, more because they don't want to hear the tale again than because they understand it.

It sometimes has to do with puns. English humor uses a lot of them. They are second nature to many people. An example happened recently when I walked into a meeting room in an

Anglican church I hadn't visited before. I asked someone who looked familiar with the place, "Is there a loo here?" "No," he said, "but there are three Roberts." That funny comment would not resonate so well in the USA, from whose people, according to Churchill, we are separated by a common language.

Secondly, a lot of humor is dependent on the way things are said. That is why jokes are better told than read. The expression on the face of the storyteller or the situation in which something happens are part of the reason for what is ridiculous having its appeal. I realized this when I went to work in the Netherlands. I had come from a culture of very dry and sarcastic humor in the west of Scotland, and presumed that that would work everywhere.

Within a week of being in Amsterdam, a girl I knew slightly asked me how I was enjoying the city. "Oh, Janeke," I said with a long face, "it's terrible. Every night I cry myself to sleep wishing I was back in Glasgow." "Well," she replied, "if you are feeling so terrible, you must telephone me and I shall come round and try to comfort you." In an attempt to avoid that at all costs, I smiled and said casually, "No. It's all right. I was only joking." At this she was not amused. "How dare you make a fool of me?" she asked. "I am concerned about your welfare and you just want to manipulate my emotions." I dropped sarcasm after that.

But there is also an "in-humor," shared in a particular community, but does not translate to other ones. An instance of that was when a friend and I shared what was called a "double bed-sit" in a student flat when we were both at Glasgow University. There were two double rooms and three singles, in one of which lived a girl called Grace who came from Nigeria and was a nursing student. Because there was no intercom system, whenever the doorbell rang whoever was in the hall opened the door and then alerted the relevant occupant that they had a visitor.

One night at the end of October as Denis and I were having dinner, the doorbell rang and Grace opened the hall door. Immediately she screamed and ran into our room protesting that she had seen a ghost. We rose from the table, went to the door and began laughing—something that made Grace worse. She had not seen a real ghost. She had experienced a Scottish Hallowe'en. While we found it funny, she—from her African background—found it very disturbing, indeed almost malign, that adults should dress up as ghosts and go from door to door on All Hallows' Evening.

Biblical puns

Keeping these things in mind, we return to the issue of humor and Jesus, and have to acknowledge that *a)* because he spoke a different language and *b)* belonged to a different culture; and *c)* because the Bible is notoriously limited in using adverbs to describe how people spoke, we may have to work hard to recognize the humor that is there.

We certainly can find puns in the Hebrew of the Old Testament and the Greek of the New. To us, Adam is a proper name with no direct association with physical terrain. But in Hebrew the word for earth is *adamah* out of which, according to Genesis, comes *Adam*. In the Gospels, we find a curious statement from Jesus about how "it is easier for a camel to pass through the eye of a needle than for a rich man to enter the kingdom of God" *(Matthew 19:24)*. It is clearly an example of hyperbole or exaggeration. But some scholars suggest that

127

there may be two less evident ambiguities. One is that it might not be a camel *(kamelos)* but a rope *(kamilos)*. Others have suggested that there was an arch in Jerusalem called the Needle's Eye, through which a camel could squeeze only with considerable indignity.

What the exact reference is we simply don't know; but it may be sufficient to note that the existence of punning in Hebrew and Greek would provide amusement for those familiar with the languages, while it is lost on those who are not.

The way he said it

When we consider the way things were said, we may—if we liberate our imaginations—come closer to the humor in Jesus. Some people may remember seeing the musical *Godspell*, the libretto or script of which was based primarily on Matthew's Gospel. In the mouth of David Essex, who played Jesus in the 1972 British premiere, words normally associated with the sombre and sepulchral ambience of dimly lit churches sparkled with fun. Particularly memorable was the way in which Essex portrayed Jesus mimicking his critics, the Pharisees, with their pretentious dignity and self-obsession as they displayed their piety in public to impress other people.

Consider a well-known incident (discussed in Chapter Four) in John's Gospel where, depending on how we read the verses, there may be mischief in Jesus' voice as well as his eyes. This is the wedding reception at Cana where his mother says to him, "They have no wine left," and he replies, "My hour has not yet come" *(John 2:3–4)*. Is this Mary anxiously interceding at her hand-wringing and servile worst? Or is this a middle-aged woman who wants the party to go on, and senses that her son might be able to ensure it? Is Jesus, in his reply, indicating that this is not the occasion on which he will initiate the Eucharist? Or is this Jesus saying the equivalent to what a young man today might mean by the words "Give me a minute, mother!"?

Several perspectives are possible, but we do no service to Jesus or Mary by constantly imagining them as the kind of permanently serious-minded individuals in whose company few people would feel at ease. Thus Craig R. Koester, in his essay from *Word, Theology, and Community in John,* ("Comedy, Humor, and the Gospel of John") comments:

> The author of John's Gospel seems to tell the story with a straight face, yet at least some interpreters have found it difficult to resist the conclusion that the evangelist had a sense of humor and that the humor is deeply consistent with the Gospel's stated purpose, which is that readers might have life in Jesus' name.

Take another example from Matthew. Here is the episode as it appears in his Gospel:

> On their arrival at Capernaum, the collectors of the temple tax came up to Peter and asked, "Does your master not pay temple tax?" "He does," said Peter. When he went indoors Jesus forestalled him by asking, "Tell me, Simon, from whom do earthly monarchs collect tribute money? From their own people, or from aliens?" "From aliens," said Peter. "Yes," said Jesus, "and their own people are exempt. But as we do not want to cause offence, go and cast a line in the lake; take the first fish

you catch, open its mouth, and you will find a silver
coin; take that and pay the tax for us both."

(Matthew 17:24–27)

What is this? A miracle story? Unlikely, both because
Jesus refuses to use his miraculous powers for personal
aggrandizement, and because the incident ends as above. All
genuine miracle stories include Jesus saying certain words
that effect a recognizable change. There is nothing here about
Peter going with his line and catching a fish with a coin of the
realm stuck in its throat. So what kind of story is this?

Years ago when my colleague Graham Maule and I shared a
youth work job we responded to some questions young people
had about Jesus by writing dialogues to help open up some
biblical passages. Here is the text of the earliest. It is called
The Silver Coin.

Peter: Eh . . . Jesus . . . ?

Jesus: Yes, Peter . . . ?

Peter: Eh . . . I've got . . .
eh . . . we've got . . .
Eh . . . I think there's a problem!

Jesus: Yes, Peter?

Peter: It's a problem about money.

Jesus: I see . . . so, what's the problem?

Peter: Eh . . . we don't have any.

Jesus: But that's nothing new, Peter.

Peter: No, Jesus.

(A pause)

Peter: Eh . . . Jesus?

Jesus: Yes, Peter?

Peter: What do you think about taxes?

Jesus: I've never been in one, Peter.

Peter: No . . . not taxis . . . *taxes!*

Jesus: Well, what do you think about them?

Peter: I worry when we don't have money to pay them.

That's the problem . . .
we're going to Capernaum . . .
when we get there,
they'll ask us to pay taxes.

And that means money . . .
And . . . and we don't have any.

Jesus: But that's nothing new, Peter.

Peter: No, Jesus.

(A pause)

Peter: Eh . . . Jesus?

Jesus: *(Getting exasperated)*
            Yes, Peter!!

Peter: What are you going to do then?

Jesus: What am I going to do then?

You mean, what are *you* going to do then!

Peter: Yes . . . I mean, what are you going to do then . . .
I mean . . . what am *I* going to do then?

Jesus: You're going to stop worrying . . .
and start fishing.

Peter: Fishing???

Jesus: That's right.

You're going to take a line and throw it in the lake.
And when you pull it out,
you'll find you've caught a big fish . . .
with a silver coin in its mouth.

Peter: Jesus, I've heard of gold fillings . . .
but this is ridiculous!

How could a fish have a silver coin in its mouth?

Jesus: Oh, it'll get one . . .
when you take it to the market . . .

It's amazing how much some folk will give
for a five-pound salmon.

Peter: *(Slowly realizing)*
Oh, I see.

Jesus: Had you not thought of that?

Peter: No, Jesus, I didn't think.

Jesus: But that's nothing new, Peter.

Peter: No, Jesus.

In-jokes

But what about humor that owes its mirth to a shared culture or experience, which outsiders might not understand?

I became aware of this kind of gospel humor in 2006 when I visited El Salvador in conjunction with Christian Aid, the British Churches' overseas development agency. The party I was with visited an area that had been devastated by a hurricane, but which recently—with financial assistance from Britain—had had a fresh water supply piped into a village for the first time. One of the local heroes who had helped to rebuild the village after the hurricane was a 14-year-old boy called Jus.

I went to visit him in his house, arguably the poorest dwelling I have ever entered on any continent. It was a tin shack with a leaking roof and no shelves or cupboards. Jus' clothes hung on strings that traversed the space. There were two beds, one used by his mother, an inebriate who was not often at home, and there were animals—dogs, two ducks and some ducklings, and a hen and two chicks that had hatched under Jus' bed the night before.

That kind of accommodation would not be too far removed from the old Black Houses on the Island of Skye in Scotland or some of the houses in Palestine at the time of Christ—a large room in which everyone lived and a bed in which the whole family slept. In Jesus' parable it is night time, when the husband is in bed with his wife and children, she perhaps sleeping at the outside so she can more easily breastfeed the baby. There are no electric lights, no paraffin lamps, no battery-operated flashlights. Domestic animals—anything from dogs to hens—may be inside and, if there are thieves about, the goat might be inside too. A sleeping menagerie.

Then someone comes to the door:

> Suppose one of you has a friend who comes to him in the middle of the night and says, "My friend, lend me three loaves, for a friend of mine on a journey has turned up at my house, and I have nothing to offer him"; and he replies from inside, "Do not bother me. The door is shut for the night; my children and I have gone to bed; and I cannot get up and give you what you want."

> I tell you that even if he will not get up and provide for him out of friendship, his very persistence will make the man get up and give him all he needs. So I say to you, ask, and you will receive; seek, and you will find; knock, and the door will be opened to you. *(Luke 11:5–9)*

Just when Jesus' listeners begin to giggle at the thought of who or what a barefooted man might tramp on between his bed and the door, Jesus lets them see the trouble that God would go to if we knock on his door.

There are many other examples of humor in the parables of Jesus, in the illustrations he gives, in the way he speaks to people, discernible if we allow him to sound like a living man and not a dead biblical hero.

If there is humor in the Bible and in Jesus, perhaps we should ask why it is there. John's Gospel—the easiest in which to find implicit humor—can provide us with the answer.

The Gospel is not:

> God so hated the world that he predestined it to eternal damnation.

The Gospel is:

God so loved the world that he gave his only Son.

(John 3:16)

The Gospel is not:

Your sins have found you out and you are henceforth banished to the furthest basement in hell.

The Gospel is:

Neither do I condemn you . . . Go; do not sin again.

(John 8:11)

The Gospel is not:

I have come that my cynicism might infect you and your despair become more profound.

The Gospel is:

I have [come] . . . that my joy may be in you, and your joy complete.

(John 15:11)

Bibliography

Books cited and/or recommended for further reading:

Honest to God
John Robinson (Westminster John Knox Press)
Jesus before Christianity
Albert Nolan (Orbis Books)
Jesus Christ Liberator: A Critical Christology for Our Times
Leonardo Boff (Orbis Books)
Jesus, the Man and the Myth: A Contemporary Christology
James P. Mackey (Paulist Press)
Social-Science Commentary on the Synoptic Gospels
Bruce J. Malina & Richard L. Rohrbaugh (Fortress Press)
Stealing Jesus: How Fundamentalizm Betrays Christianity
Bruce Bawer (Three Rivers Press)
The Cambridge Companion to Jesus
ed. Markus Bockmuehl (Cambridge University Press)
The Cost of Discipleship
Dietrich Bonhoeffer (SCM Press)
The Gospel in Art by the Peasants of Solentiname
ed. Philip & Sally Scharper (Orbis Books)
The Meaning of Jesus: Two Visions
Marcus J. Borg & N. T. Wright (HarperOne)
The Politics of Jesus
John Howard Yoder (Wm. B. Eerdmans Publishing)
What Jesus Meant
Garry Wills (Viking Press)
Word, Theology, and Community in John
ed. John Painter, R. Alan Culpepper, Fernando F. Segovia
(Chalice Press)

The Wild Goose Resource Group

The Wild Goose Resource Group is an expression of the Iona Community's commitment to the renewal of public worship. Based in Glasgow, the WGRG has two resource workers, John Bell and Graham Maule, and a project worker, Jamie Schmeling, who lead workshops, seminars and events throughout Britain and abroad. They are supported by Gail Ullrich (administrator) and Victoria Rudebark (sales & copyright administrator).

From 1984 to 2001, the WGRG workers were also part of the Wild Goose Worship Group. The WGWG consisted of around sixteen, predominantly lay, people at any one time, who came from a variety of occupational and denominational backgrounds. Over the 17 years of its existence, it was the WGWG who tested, as well as promoted, the material in this book.

The task of both groups has been to develop and identify new methods and materials to enable the revitalisation of congregational song, prayer and liturgy. The songs and liturgical material have now been translated and used in many countries across the world as well as being frequently broadcast on radio and television.

The WGRG, along with a committed group of fellow-Glaswegians, run HOLY CITY, a monthly ecumenical workshop and worship event for adults in the centre of Glasgow. The WGRG also publishes a mail-order catalogue, an annual Liturgy Booklet series and a twice-yearly newsletter, GOOSEgander, to enable friends and supporters to keep abreast of WGRG developments. If you would like to find out more about subscribing to these, or about ways to support the WGRG financially, please contact:

The Wild Goose Resource Group, Iona Community,
Fourth Floor, Savoy House, 140 Sauchiehall Street,
Glasgow G2 3DH, Scotland.
Tel: 0141 332 6343   Fax: 0141 332 1090

e-mail: wgrg@gla.iona.org.uk   web: www.iona.org.uk/wgrg
www.wgrg.co.uk   www.holycity-glasgow.co.uk

Wild Goose Publications is part of
The Iona Community:

- An ecumenical movement of men and women from different walks of life and different traditions in the Christian church
- Committed to the gospel of Jesus Christ, and to following where that leads, even into the unknown
- Engaged together, and with people of goodwill across the world, in acting, reflecting and praying for justice, peace and the integrity of creation
- Convinced that the inclusive community we seek must be embodied in the community we practise

Together with our staff, we are responsible for:

- Our islands residential centres of Iona Abbey, the MacLeod Centre on Iona, and Camas Adventure Centre on the Ross of Mull

and in Glasgow:

- The administration of the Community
- Our work with young people
- Our publishing house, Wild Goose Publications
- Our association in the revitalising of worship with the Wild Goose Resource Group

The Iona Community was founded in Glasgow in 1938 by George MacLeod, minister, visionary and prophetic witness for peace, in the context of the poverty and despair of the Depression. Its original task of rebuilding the monastic ruins of Iona Abbey became a sign of hopeful rebuilding of community in Scotland and beyond. Today, we are about 250 members, mostly in Britain, and 1500 associate members, with 1400 friends worldwide. Together and apart, 'we follow the light we have, and pray for more light'.

For information on the Iona Community contact:
The Iona Community,
Fourth Floor, Savoy House, 140 Sauchiehall Street,
Glasgow G2 3DH, UK.
Phone: 0141 332 6343
e-mail: admin@iona.org.uk; web: www.iona.org.uk

For enquiries about visiting Iona, please contact:
Iona Abbey, Isle of Iona, Argyll PA76 6SN, UK.
Phone: 01681 700404
e-mail: ionacomm@iona.org.uk

For more information on publications by John L. Bell,
the Iona Community,
and the Wild Goose Resource Group,
please contact:

GIA Publications, Inc.
giamusic.com/bios/iona